Toon P
Public Houses In & Around Newcastle upon Tyne

Paul Chrystal

DestinWorld
publishing

'I would give all of my fame for a pot of ale and safety.'

William Shakespeare, (fl. c. 1585–1613)
- Henry V, Henry V, Act III, Scene 2,

'The pub is the heart of England'.

- Samuel Pepys (1633–1703)

'there is nothing which has yet been contrived by man, by which so much happiness is produced, as by a good tavern or inn'.

- Samuel (Dr) Johnson (1709 – 1784)

First Edition 2023

ISBN 978 1 83800 867 3

British Library Cataloguing–in–Publication Data
A catalogue record for this book is available from the British Library.

Published by Destinworld Publishing Ltd.
www.destinworld.com

Printed and bound in Bulgaria

Printed on FSC® and PEFC certified paper from responsibly managed forests.

Cover image:
'The Pubs of Newcastle', by Ben Staves.
Courtesy of and ©Ben Staves.
Staves Art www.stavesart.com @stavesart

About the author

Paul Chrystal was educated at the universities of Hull and Southampton, where he took degrees in Classics.

More recently he has been history advisor to Yorkshire visitor attractions, writing features for national newspapers, and broadcasting on talkRADIO, History Hack, BBC local radio, on Radio 4's PM programme and on the BBC World Service.

He is contributor to a number of history and archaeology magazines and the author of the best-selling *A History of Britain in 100 Objects (2022)*.

He is past editor of *York History,* journal of the York Archaeological & York Architectural Society and of *Yorkshire Archaeological Journal*. His books have been translated into Chinese and Japanese.

I had a pint of this in the Broad Chare; did the trick

Acknowledgements

A book like this is always a joint enterprise between the author and the personalities in his book – in this case the landladies and landlords, managers, hosts and hostesses of the one hundred or so pubs, bars, inns and beer houses included. Without their help the book would be deficient in many ways and would be just another arid listing of places to go for a drink.

So, I would like to thank the following, in no particular order, for their help and contributions:

Thanks to Stephen Innes and Trudy Kepke, www.artthroughalens.co.uk, for permission to use the Broad Chare image. To Alastair Gilmour, Cheers North East for permission to quote from the article on the Crown Posada murals (www. cheersnortheast.co.uk/jewels-in-the-crown/. Ben Staves @stavesart was kind enough to give permission to use the Pubs in Newcastle artwork on the cover.

Thanks also to Yvette Earl at Yvette Earl Illustration for permission to reproduce the images of the Central Bar, Gateshead and the Tyne Bar in Ouseburn. To see more of Yvette's splendid work visit www. yvette-earl.com.

Ian Johnson at the Robinson Library Special Collections, Newcastle University kindly gave permission for me to use the image of the Crown Temperance Hotel Accession number: ILL/11/188 Robinson Library Newcastle University, Newcastle University Special Collections, GB 186.

'The Landlord' by F.W. Elwell (1870–1958), in Ferens Art Gallery, Hull.

Percy Anderson was landlord of the British Queen in Gateshead; he would have looked very like the Landlord in the Ferens Gallery. Percy was brother to Tot from the Old Nag's Head. 'He is remembered by his granddaughter Joyce Robson as being immaculately and formally dressed with pin-striped trousers, white apron, starched collar and beautifully polished shoes. This would have been the norm for landlords whose task it was to set a good example and maintain order'. [Boothroyd, Gateshead p. 12]

Thanks as well to Marie-Louise Mackay at the Cameron's Heritage Centre, Hartlepool for permission to use information and images - https://cameronsbrewery.com/.

In addition number of books and websites have been enormously helpful; they include:

Brian Bennison's numerous books; Lynn Pearson's, *The Northumbrian Pub - an architectural history*; John Boothroyd, *The Old Pubs of Gateshead*, Andrew Clark, *Newcastle's Old Pubs Remembered*, and *The Newcastle Chronicle*.

www.whatpub.com; CAMRA; JD Wetherspoon; www.pubsgalore.co.uk; https://co-curate.ncl.ac.uk/; and what others have to say at Pubs Galore - The UK Pub Guide.

Same author

Pubs in & around the Yorkshire Dales

Pubs in & around York

Hull Pubs

Leeds Pubs

Harrogate & Knaresborough pubs

The Place names of Yorkshire…some pubs too

The Place names of County Durham

The Place names of Northumberland (in press)

The Romans in the North

For a full list please go to www.paulchrystal.com
Unless acknowledged otherwise all text
is ©Paul Chrystal

Contents

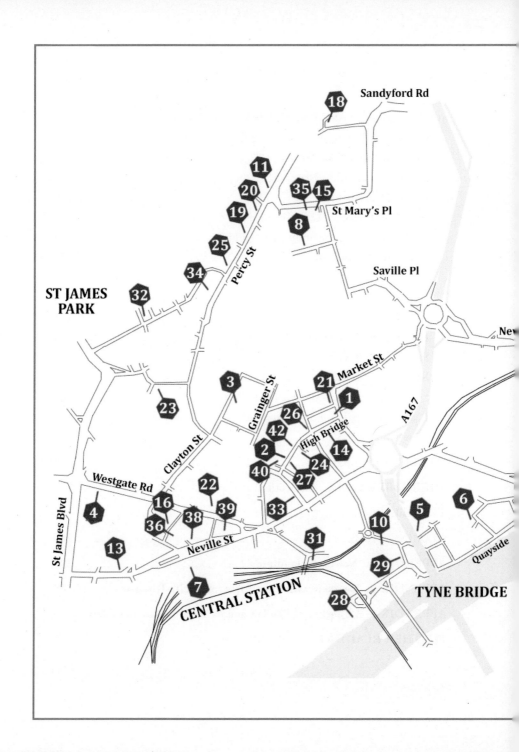

NEWCASTLE PUBS

St

y Rd

Walker Rd

GATESHEAD PUBS

1 The Barley Mow
2 The British Lion
3 The Central Bar
4 The Grey Nag's Head
5 The Metropole
6 The Old Nag's Head
7 The Queen's Head
8 The Schooner
9 Station East
10 The Tilley Stone

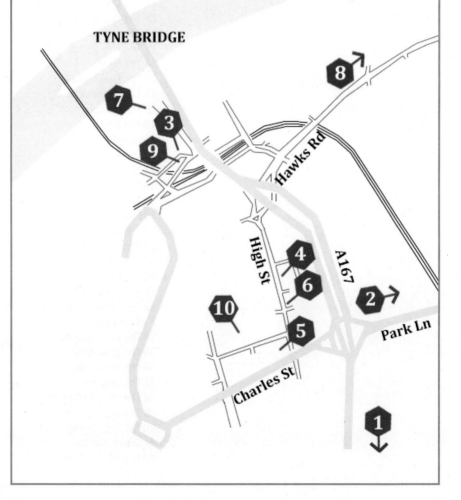

TYNE BRIDGE

The Tyne Bar. courtesy of and copyright Yvette Earl

OPENING TIME

I n the days before that lifesaver, the SatNav, the hopelessly lost car, white van
or coach driver would pull over, wind down his or her window and call over
to an unsuspecting local and ask for directions to his or her destination. The
response – usually impossibly overcomplicated but well-meaning for all that –
would inevitably involve 'turning left at the church and then right at the pub' or
a variation thereof. The pub, like the church, is often a constant, a given in every
village or town or city centre or suburb, a symbol of foreverness, reassurance and
permanence; the ubiquity of pubs and their crucial role in community life seemed
always to have been there, to enjoy and to savour. As was and is the beer, ale, mild
or stout to be had there. Indeed, one line in the Kinks' 1968 *We are the Village
Green Preservation Society* – that anthem of a lost English past – runs 'We are the
Draught Beer Preservation Society', along with Desperate Dan and the Custard
Pie Appreciation Consortium, and many more revered old-English institutions.

A host of pubs have been named after George Orwell's 1946 description of
his ideal pub in the fictitious "Moon Under Water", which concludes in what is
unadulterated nostalgia before nostalgia was invented:

> *'And if anyone knows of a pub that has draught stout, open fires, cheap
> meals, a garden, motherly barmaids and no radio, I should be glad to hear
> of it, even though its name were something as prosaic as the Red Lion or
> the Railway Arms'.*

This book is a practical beer drinker's guide to lots of the public houses in
and around the wonderful city of Newcastle-upon-Tyne, a city made all the more
wonderful by the very pubs this book describes. Where possible, for each pub
I describe its history, the origin of its name and previous names, and relevant
(printable) anecdotes. As with my previous books on pubs, *Toon Pubs* is itself

a bit like a good pub: accessible, friendly and rewarding with the promise of good beer. *Toon Pubs* is, in short, an engaging guide to the pubs of Newcastle and its environs. The book is 'practical' because the maps show you how to get there (and back); I give addresses, post codes (for SatNav), phone numbers, e mail and websites (where they exist), and I point out anything special to look for once you're there. Most pubs have a unique story to tell so, where possible, the history and development of these pubs is described with information on its origins, the clientele they were built to cater for, significant events they witnessed, how the pubs got their names or what the names signify, anecdotes about them and about characters who may have drunk – or got drunk – in them.

Toon Pubs is, then, an informative and fascinating practical guide for anyone strolling in and around Newcastle or Gateshead (or indeed further afield) - two of England's finest, most historical and diverse cities - who has a bit of time on their hands and wants to learn some local history in the most convivial of ways. The history they are likely to pick up in the book is often oblique and unusual; it will, nevertheless, convey a compelling sense of the history of Newcastle and its surrounding conurbations.

How does that happen? Pubs, like the names of towns and villages, hills, rivers and dales, often tell us much about local history in the vicinity, famous local people and local topography.

The book continues with a sad chapter on Newcastle and Gateshead's lost pubs - a selection of some of the more interesting ex-pubs with a tale to tell. Those that are long gone are just as eloquent about the past as those whose doors remain open. The north east's brewing industry past and present is surveyed; breweries, of course, are inseparable from the pubs they serve and an important strand of social and economic history of the north east of England. The recent explosion of pubs serving real ale and craft beers, and of micro-pubs and microbreweries, is a very welcome antidote to the creeping demise of the public house on the high street and town square.

Many of the older pubs we cover are, by definition, more interestingly historically with a tale or two to tell in their long histories. As Lynn Pearson reminds us in her highly informative *The Northumbrian Pub: An Architectural History* (p. 9)

> *'The surviving pubs built in the late Victorian and early Edwardian building boom are not merely buildings but constant reminders of fashionable artistic taste, of high quality craft skills, of architectural showmanship and crucially, of the great investment made by the brewing industry in buildings as a means of attracting customers'.*

To Lynn Pearson (and many others) north east pubs are different, say, from the grand Victorian pubs of London and the terracotta pubs of Birmingham - and that difference is forged by the social and economic vicissitudes experienced locally in Newcastle, Hartlepool, Middlesbrough or Sunderland, for example. But there is more to the pub than that. Very often they give an insight into the character of the area in which they serve their customers, giving us a view through an unerring lens of the local demographic, industry, commerce, employment, sporting events, arts and entertainment, relative wealth and poverty, domestic set up and crime.

For the sake of balance the important story of temperance is covered, particularly where it relates to Tyneside, since this is an essential part of social history and, like brewing, is inextricably associated with any regions' drinking culture.

Times have changed since as recently as the beginning of the 21st century even: then the average adult drank 218 pints per person; by 2011, that same adult downed just 152 pints, a 30pc drop*. In 2002 there were 60,100 pubs in the UK; there were approximately 46,800 pubs operating in the United Kingdom in 2020. This represented a decrease of approximately 8,600 pubs in the last ten years, and a decline of over 14,000 pubs since 2000 according to CAMRA**.

A report in *The Times* in 2022 will surprise anyone who has been in Bigg Market on a Friday or Saturday night; it is entitled 'Pub visits go dry as young snub booze' (July 18 2022) by Tom Ball who alerts us to the fact that 'no alcohol is drunk in almost a third of all trips to the pub amid a trend towards temperance that is being driven by the young'. Around 29 per cent pub visits and 37 per cent of restaurant meals are now entirely dry according to a report by KAM, the hospitality research company. Health concerns are one of the key drivers in this trend. The proportion of non-drinkers has increased by three per cent since 2015 according to Drink Aware: seventeen per cent of men and twenty-two per cent of women drink no drink. Surprisingly perhaps 'the least likely to drink are aged between 16 and 24 with 26 per cent of that group teetotal'. On the other hand, those most predisposed to a drink are in the 55 to 74 age group with fifteen per cent teetotal. A desire to cut down on alcohol consumption due to health concerns and a desire to enjoy other forms of leisure are given by 55 per cent, rising to 65 per cent amongst drinkers in their twenties and late teens. Money, of course, is another factor, even though the government insists that 'alcohol is 74 per cent more affordable now than in 1987'. They may want to revise that in the wake of the ongoing cost of living crisis and the increase in duty on some alcoholic drinks on August 1, 2023#.

Non-alcoholic beer and lager is, thankfully, much more palatable these days and some brewers can report like-for-like growth of 180 per cent since January 2021. Despite this I can still go into a pub when I'm driving only to find no alcoholic beers on sale at all. Wake up!

Figures for Germany published by the World Health Organisation in 2019 show that average annual consumption per capita has dropped from 1.14 litres to 12.9 since 2000.

Britain is 23rd in the 2019 world beer consumption league table:

Great Britain consumption per capita, litres per year: 70.3 or 123 pints; 2018 change: - 1.4 litres per year; total national consumption, million litres per year: 4,712

Czech Republic is #1 with 140 litres per capita; Indonesia is #61 with 0.7 litres per capita ***.

While a reduction in our beer consumption must be wholeheartedly welcomed for personal and public health reasons, it is the inexorable decline in the number of pubs where adults can drink responsibly and sociably that is a cause for concern, not least for social, psychological and wellbeing reasons. The closures have, of course, been amplified by the ravages of COVID-19. The number of English and Welsh pubs fell below 40,000 for the first time during the first half of 2022, having fallen by 7,107 in the past 10 years, new research from real estate adviser Altus Group has revealed. And remember, you can always go into a pub and enjoy a good meal and usually an alcohol-free drink. Increasingly, well-behaved children and dogs are more than welcome.

Finally, just as any good pub worth its hops has a programme of guest beers, so then shall this book feature a 'guest pub'. A pub that is not actually in Newcastle but which would grace any village, town or city with its unique atmosphere and ambience, exuding everything that is just right about an English pub. That guest pub, this surrogate Toon pub, is the Dun Cow in, dare I say it, Sunderland.

*   telegraph.co.uk/finance/newsbysector/retailandconsumer/11283995/The-real-reasons-for-the-tragic-demise-of-the-British-pub-industry.html
** www.beerandpub.com/statistics
*** wikipedia.org/wiki/List_of_countries_by_beer_consumption_per_capita
#   As announced at Spring Budget 2023, the government will increase the duty rates under the revised duty structure for alcohol products being introduced from 1 August 2023 in line with the Retail Price Index (RPI). This includes all alcoholic products produced in, or imported into, the UK.
#   The government will also increase the value of Draught Relief from 5% to 9.2% for qualifying beer and cider products and from 20% to 23% for qualifying wine, other fermented products (previously made-wine) and spirits. https://www.gov.uk/government/publications/changes-to-alcohol-duty-rates/alcohol-duty-rate-changes

I hope that the wealth of detail relating to many of the pubs included will educate and entertain in equal measure and, at the same time, give the reader, an oblique and unusual but nevertheless compelling history of Newcastle and its surroundings.

Pubs have been the past and they can be the future, if we collectively get off the bloody sofa and head for the nearest hostelry. Innovative and hospitable landlords, craft and real ale local brewers, and appreciative, enthusiastic customers are the way forward. But don't take it from me - in the words of an ever - cautionary Hilaire Belloc (1870 –1953)

When you have lost your inns drown your empty selves for you will have lost the last of England.

And *the destroying hand of progress* is how T.P. Cooper1897, in *the Old Inns and Inn Signs of York* – eloquently and acidly described demolitions and changes of use - the death knell for many a pub, so often the victim of myopic and often plain stupid corporation and council decision makers, even today.

Finally, G. K. Chesterton (1874-1936) had the right idea:
[Now] will someone take me to a pub?

Having a good laugh on a girls' night out. See p 204 below

INTRODUCTION

In the 1960s and 1970s there were an estimated 75,000 pubs in the UK. Today that number is less than 40,000, according to a report by Bloomberg. As pub closures remain an issue for many UK villages, towns and cities, a new study has shown the North East is one of the UK's top regions for the number of pubs staying open.

The latest research by finance specialists RIFT reveals that some parts of Britain have seen as many as 69 local pubs close their doors in the past two years, a situation that could be made even worse when the freeze on alcohol tax ended on 1st August. RIFT continues the good news: 'Compared to the national average, which has seen a 0.3% rise in pubs between July 2020 and February 2022, the North East has seen a stunning 6.2% rise in pubs attracting customers through their doors throughout the week. The rise has been helped by situations in County Durham and Newcastle, which have seen 37 and 30 pubs open over the time frame respectively. In total the North East has 69 more pubs at the start of 2023 compared to July 2022.

So, if there is a message to take away from this book it is simply to put the book down, get up, go out and call in at your local for a pint or two and help preserve and extend this most British of social institutions. Once the pub, your favourite pub, has gone, it's often gone for good.

Just to give an example of how early pubs operated and for what clientele, Yorkshire's first pub was the ale house in which Samuel Ellis started brewing in AD 953 at Bardsey to the north of Leeds; it has survived to this day under the guise first of the Priest's Inn and then of the Bingley Arms; but the tradition and heritage started by Ellis and the Kirkstall Abbey monks who drank there on the way to St Mary's Abbey in York must be preserved. History cries out from the pub with its monastic tradition, its role as a courthouse, its pillory and its post-Reformation priest hole. Beer was being brewed and drank here in the days of King Canute (990-1035).

The Old George is reputed to be Newcastle's oldest pub, stretching back to 1582. Charles I was once a regular enjoying a pre-execution pint or two while kept prisoner in Newcastle.

In a very significant way, the history of the pub and inn – what J.B. Priestly (1894-1984) called 'a haunt of rare souls' - is the history of the city, town, village or region. People figure large in the book – without them, of course, there would be no pubs, so it is fitting that they take centre stage whether as landlords, customers, coroners, alewives, murderers, mistresses, ladies of the night or maids. In the pubs featured there is often someone colourful and interesting not very far away who has tainted, tinged or influenced the history of the establishment at one time or another.

Brewsters

In the early days, pubs brewed their own ale in small brew houses adjacent to the pub; women did much of the work, certainly before the mid-14th century Black Death: Madam Bradley of Northallerton and Nanny Driffield of Easingwold

A brewhouse in action. Despite the fact that the modern beer pump, or tap, had been invented over 100 years previously, this pair are still taking their beer the traditional way, pouring it into a glass from a jug outside the "Brew House". They are surrounded by the wooden barrels that the alcohol would have been stored in. Photograph Collection Number 675 Museum of Hartlepool. No known copyright restrictions.

are legendary; "Brewsters," or "alewives" brewed in the home for both domestic consumption and small scale commercial sale.

These brewsters made a substantial and important contribution to the family income. It was the good ale which drew neighbours into the houses of brewsters and led to the birth of the public house. Some women continued to brew into the 17th century; ale-conners routinely tested the quality of ale in order to maintain standards. Stingo, Knockerdown and Rumtum were famous Yorkshire brews with reputations as far south as London's Marylebone. Hopped ale was introduced from Flanders around 1400 after which time hops were grown in England for beer production: ale usually has a lower hop content than beer.

Apart from these domestic enterprises hostelries were set up by the roadside or at the gateways to cities catering for travellers. This began with the Romans locating *tabernae* on their extensive road network, not least in the northeast with the supply routes leading to and from Hadrian's Wall and the numerous defensive forts south of the wall. This continued with merchants plodding to and from market, drovers, commercial travellers, monks moving from monastery to monastery, pilgrims (as exemplified by Chaucer's *Canterbury Tales*) and other people moving from village to village or from town to town. The landowners and lords of the manor sometimes provided refreshing and sustaining beer house facilities for the workers in their fields. Ale was an important part of the medieval English diet being as it was affordable and clean compared to cholera and e coli ridden water. It is estimated that the average adult quaffed up to eight pints a day.

But it was not all good news. Brewsters were often scapegoats for the vices associated with the production and consumption of alcohol. In 1540, the city of Chester decreed that no women between the ages of fourteen and forty would be allowed to sell ale, with the aim of limiting the trade to women above or below the age of sexual desirability. Women who brewed and sold ale were allegedly notorious for being disobedient to their husbands, sexually deviant, cheating their customers with watered-down ale and charging extortionate prices. It was of course men – arrogant officials or wingeing punters - who pedaled such a stereotype. The Skipton Quarter Sessions of 1681 reveal early day license regulation abuse when nine Harrogate 'alehousekeepers' (four of whom were women) *did illegally, obstinately, and without licence... keep common Alehouses and Tipleing houses and there for the whole time did sell beer & ale*. From this we might assume that there were ale-selling alehouses in profusion, different from the inns and taverns which offered board and lodging, beer and wine, different with different clienteles. Nationally, in 1577, England had one alehouse for every 150 citizens; Harrogate, then, was seriously over-alehoused in 1681 as its population did not approach 15,000 until 1800. Before the fuss at Skipton, Marmaduke Mathew, Constable of Harrogate for 1637, talks of 'brewsters and innkeepers' being arraigned for serving partridges and the like during lent.

Coaching

The 17th century saw the first big change in the role of pubs when in 1657 the establishment of turnpikes, essentially taxed roads, allowed a huge increase in the number of horses and coaches criss-crossing the country. Just as the Romans set up a sophisticated network of *mansiones* for the comfort and resupply of horses and people along the empire-wide *cursus publicus,* so turnpikes demanded coaching inns for board and lodge for drivers and passengers, and stabling and veterinary services for the horses which required changing frequently, (essentially hotels). For example, in 1569 the Crown in Harrogate was the manor house of the aptly named Boroughbridge MP William Tankard and became one of the premier coaching inns on the route from York to Newcastle. In the 1780s a man called Gilbertson, landlord of the Queen's Head in Leeds, started a service from Leeds to Newcastle via Harrogate; the 'Defence' and 'High Flyer' both called at Knaresborough and Boroughbridge *en route* from Harrogate to Newcastle.

In Newcastle itself, the Turf in Collingwood Street was one of the main stopping points to and from all points in England, Scotland and Wales, notably London and Edinburgh. The journey inevitably involved a night stay in Newcastle or nearby and that stay, more often than not, was at the Turf. In 1824 local directories tell us that three coaches ran daily from the Turf to London, two to Edinburgh and one each to Carlisle, Lancaster and Leeds. The Turf closed and was demolished in 1889; a bank was erected on the site.

Newcastle's first mail coaching inn, however, was the Cock Inn which, from 1786, received and dispatched mail to and from London and Edinburgh via one coach per week. At a restricted seven miles per hour the journey to London took forty-five long, bumpy hours. The Cock was demolished in 1870 when it was replaced by a new purpose-built Post Office.

Edwin Pratt's *A History of Inland Transport and Communication in England* (chapter 24, 'End of the Coaching Era') puts the origin of coaching houses into historical context for us, showing just how important these establishment were.

'In the palmy days of Newcastle coaching - from about 1825 to 1834, there would have been a fine array of coaches opposite the Turf Hotel, the horses in teams of grey, black and bay. The Turf Hotel continued to afford accommodation for guests who found it necessary to stay overnight, until 1847, when the York and North Midland Railway to Newcastle was opened. The coaches to the south soon ceased to run, but those to Edinburgh were continued for some time longer. All the famous old inns on the Great North Road were closed one after another until none was left. Of course, the Turf suffered, but it had a good name and managed to survive the loss of custom through the advent of the iron horse.

By 1820 the improvements in road-making of Telford and McAdam had led to quicker travelling and the running of far more coaches, at greater speeds, than had previously been the case. By 1836 it was evident that coaching had reached the climax of its popularity and could not hope to maintain its position against the competition of the railways which were spreading so rapidly throughout the land.

Over 3,000 coaches were then on the road, and half of these began or ended their journeys in London. Some 150,000 horses were employed in running them, and there were about 30,000 coachmen, guards, horse-keepers and hostlers, while many hundreds of taverns, in town or country, prospered on the patronage the coaches brought them. From one London tavern alone there went every day over eighty coaches to destinations in the north. From another there went fifty-three coaches and fifty-one wagons, chiefly to the west of England. Altogether coaches or wagons were going from over one hundred taverns in the City or in the Borough.

Big interests grew up in connection with the coaching enterprise. William Chaplin, who owned five yards in London, had, at one time, nearly 2,000 horses, besides many coaches. Out of twenty-seven mail-coaches leaving London every night he "horsed" fourteen. He is said to have made a fortune of half a million of money out of the business; but when he began to realise what the locomotive would do he took his coaches off the road, disposed of his stock before the railways had depreciated it, joined with Benjamin Horne, of the "Golden Cross," Charing Cross, who had himself had a large stock of horses, and founded the carrying firm of Chaplin and Horne, which became exclusive agents for the London and Birmingham Railway.

As for Gateshead, the coaching inn of choice was the Black Bull in the High Street with its twenty rooms and stabling for 100 horses – but there were others, the equestrian signage maybe betraying their business: The Old Nag's Head; Grey Horse and Grey Nag's Head. And then there was the Coach and Horses, another stopping place at 76 High Street for the mail coach until 1844; it was known as Red Robin's because landlord Robert Stephenson wore a smart red waistcoat with his publican's apron. His son, Robert, ran the Three Tons and sported the same attire so the pub became Red Bob. The night Robert disturbed a burglar ended in tragedy when he was clubbed to death with his own crutch.

The Railways

The next major development, as Pratt says, came with the railways 200 years later and the establishment of railway inns at stations; the third was the now ubiquitous car and the need to cater for day trippers, business people, commuters and other travellers – often in the very pubs which once served weary coach and railway passengers.

Brewers

The first common brewers were the Nesfield family of Scarborough established in 1691. But it was the end of the 18th century which saw the emergence of the common brewery; this was boosted by the Beerhouse Act in 1830, with names from the 19th century like Camerons, Theakstons, Wylam, Scottish & Newcastle, John Smith's and Sam Smith's all still very much alive today. The aim of the 1830 Act was to encourage people to drink beer rather than spirits. Any householder who paid the poor rate could sell beer, ale or porter by buying an excise license but did not a need justices' licence; spirit selling retailers did. The beer-sellers had to promise to give correct measures, maintain good order, to allow no drunkenness or gambling and not to dilute the beer! Hmmm… However, the Act backfired: many beer houses emerged from the back streets of large cities and became working class drinking dens. *The Leeds Mercury* of 23rd October 1830 reported, "We receive from many quarters grievous complaints of the demoralising effects of this Act, which has, by making beer cheap, led to an increase of intoxication".

Morality Issues

Beer, and drinking alcohol generally, can of course breed and attract vice, and corporations agonised and wrung their collective hands similarly over morality and prostitution, a trade exaggerated in Newcastle and Gateshead with its transitory population of seamen, soldiers, travellers and prostitutes who were seen as a serious threat to local morality. Pubs, where these itinerants gathered, just fostered this. Unmarried mothers were dealt with severely – drinking being blamed for their immorality; and on one occasion at least, women were even threatened penalties for wearing extravagant clothes by the legal authorities. Things are unlikely to have improved at the close of the 17th century when social life was partly influenced by the Society for the Reformation of Manners, which campaigned energetically against swearing and drunkenness.

Indeed, Newcastle, in common with other ports, in a bid to reduce immoral behaviour, enjoyed the beneficence and diversions on offer from various institutions – institutions which we might term charitable organisations today; some were educational, some philanthropic: to name a few there were the Ragged schools, the Mechanics' Institute, the Young People's Christian and Literary Institute, the Sailors' Home and Sailors' Institute, the Hull and East Riding Penitentiary for Fallen Women, the Temporary Home for Fallen Women, and other such societies like the Society for the Relief of Really Deserving Foreigners, a society we would do well to revive today. But Newcastle life was Newcastle life: the good works had to battle against the gig economy: casual labour in the docks, seasonal employment in shipping, fishing, smuggling. According to T.H. Travis, a stipendiary magistrate in Hull, there were 306 brothels known to the police in 1869. For most Hull people the only opportunities for fun and entertainment recreation were Hull Fair once a year and the 309 gin-shops and 287 beer houses thriving in the town in 1869, and those brothels. Newcastle's experience would have been much the same.

Wellington's Beerhouse Act of 1830 saw licensed premises double in ten years with 25,000 new licenses issued within three months of the legislation. It also galvanised the rise and rise of the common brewery, brewing beer and selling it to other outlets rather than for oneself. In 1823 Hull had 274 inns serving a population of 44,924 making one pub per 164 people; York was even better provisioned with 194 inns for 22,529 inhabitants: one for every 116 residents. Take children out of the demographic and the figures are even more astonishing. Tadcaster takes the biscuit in 1837 with twenty-four inns and taverns and eleven beer houses: thirty-five places to drink for a population of 2,400 providing one pub for every seventy people – more than twice the national average at the time. At its peak Sheffield in 1863 had 560 inns and hotels with 682 beer houses and over 600 off licences. Beerhouses naturally proliferated around the steel mills and heavy engineering factories: a common sight was boys wielding broomsticks with cans suspended full of beer for the delectation of dusty and thirsty workers.

By the late 1880s the practice of pubs brewing their own beer had declined significantly with only 10 per cent of publicans brewing their own beer; by 1891 in all of Tyneside there were only three publicans who held a licence to brew.

The early years of this century has seen the welcome rise of the microbrewery and artisan breweries, for example Anarchy Brew Co., Box Social Brewing, Tyne Bank Brewery and Tap Room and Microbus.

Themed Pubs and Pub Names

Some pubs now are tastefully themed, like the Left Luggage Room and Pumphreys; others exude history, notably Crown Posada and the Redhouse; others still can boast fascinating names like the Microchimp and the Strawberry with their own stories to tell. Animals are everywhere to be seen: the ubiquitous Red Lion (457 in the UK and the most popular); White Hart (239, fourth); White Horse (196, seventh) and the Swan (174, tenth) – as well as numerous names of racehorses have seen to that. An example is the Beeswing in Felling, a horse which wone 51 races including the Ascot Gold Cup in 1842, the Doncaster Cup (four times) and the Newcastle Cup (six times).

Gateshead had its Goat and two nags: the Old Nag's Head (Top Nag's), the Grey Nag's Head (bottom Nag's), as well as a Grey Horse. Three different pubs certainly but were they all the same horse? Newcastle, too, has a Goat. Hull's Goat and Compasses is a corruption of the Puritan motto 'God encompasses us'. The Squinting Cat in Pannal near Harrogate gets its delightful name from a former landlady known as 't'owd cat': she was in the habit of squinting out of the window from behind the curtains to scrutinize customers as they approached; in doing so she gave the pub it's nickname, the Cat. So, in 1930 when the pub was refurbished it was renamed the Squinting Cat. Similar, but different, is the Blinking Owl at Boroughbridge. And then there was the Dun Cow on Gateshead High Street with its famous ceiling, formerly the Red Cow – a product of sheer fantasy, with at least sixteen more known in England. Locally, other Dun Cows graze peacefully in Durham city, Sedgefield, Stockton-on-Tees and Houghton-le-Spring. Legend has it that the Dun Cow in Dunchurch was a "monstrous beast four yards high and six yards long" which provided milk to the locals. A witch made it go on a murderous rampage until it was slain by Guy, Earl of Warwick. Coincidentally in 1605, the Gunpowder plotters also stayed in Dunchurch, Warwickshire. Dun is a dull shade of brownish grey. As for the red cow name, Richards and Curl in 1973 (*City of London Pubs: A Practical and Historical Guide*) say of Old Red Cow at 71-72 Long Lane, London EC1 "The origin of this name is simplicity itself, as old red cows are a rare sight in this country, it follows that their milk (beer) is of great value."

The menagerie is complemented by the Gorilla (later the Phoenix), Mallard, Eagle and Black Bull, Old Fox, Fox and Lamb, Flying Horse, Swan, Talbot (also coffin dealers), Greenland Bear, White Bear, and Bay Horse – all in Gateshead with the Buck in Low Fell. The Cuckoo – a nickname for the King's Arms – was in Newcastle as was the Nightingale Tavern in Churchill Street, Lamb's Hotel (Lamb & Flag), the Black Bull, the Black Bulls Head and the Hare's Nest. The Foresters' Arms in Derwentwater Road was nicknamed the Coffin – possibly for the same reason as the Talbot. There aren't many pubs named after butterflies but the Azure Blue in Bensham is one - the original name was going to be the Painted Lady! On the same theme the Wickham House is often called the Wicked House. Sadly in 1994 the then landlord of the Azure Blue, George Gill, was murdered. Better known as Vivian he was formerly the landlord of the Crown in Coatsworth Road. Still on biology names there was a Honeysuckle Hotel with its marble front and domed tower; the Prince of Wales in Hampden Street often went by the name, the Hen and Chicks.

Astronomically, the Seven Stars in Pleiad Place is named after the Pleiades constellation, visible with the naked eye. More bizarrely, though, the pub was the haunt of pigeon fanciers run by an eccentric former mariner who kept a monkey behind the bar captured on his travels. In Newcastle we have a Durham Ox, Falcon (the Bonny Bird), and a Golden Eagle, all in the Scotswood Road. The Durham Ox (March 1796 – 15 April 1807) was a steer who became famous in the early 19th century for his shape, size and weight. He was an early example of the Shorthorn breed of cattle and helped establish the standards by which the breed was to be defined. He became known as the Ketton Ox when he was exhibited in Darlington in 1799. In 1801 the ox was sold to John Day of Harmston, near Lincoln, for £250 (2010: £14,900), who renamed him the Durham Ox and had a carriage specially made to transport him, drawn by four horses. For the next five years the ox toured with him around England and Scotland, being exhibited to the public at agricultural fairs and other events.

Pub Signs

Pub signs and the names and the images on them are an intriguing subject all of their own. The Romans started it all with a sign depicting a bunch of vine leaves to denote a *taberna*. There is a belief that vine leaves were in relatively short supply (we were never known for locally produced wine or dolmades), so instead, they hung bushes up and this is what inspired the first pub names,

such as The Hollybush, The Bull & Bush and The Bush. As with any other commercial enterprise pubs used signs or symbols to signify the nature of the business undertaken within.

We are all familiar with old business branding and signage such as the ubiquitous barber's pole and the pawnbroker's balls which survive to this day; in York rarer examples exist like the native red Indian denoting a tobacconists; the statue of Minerva (goddess of wisdom) indicating a bookshop, and the bible outside what was another bookshop; a statue of Napoleon Bonaparte nonchalantly rolling snuff was the welcoming sign of a York tobacconists. The reason for all this symbolism was that most people were illiterate until the end of the 19th century, so words would have been useless: a sign, however, spoke volumes. From 1393 it was obligatory for innkeepers to display a sign: pubs accordingly created names and signs to indicate and differentiate: the sign set it apart from other inns and taverns in the locality; it also advertised what might be found inside, or indeed the political persuasion of the landlord. Coats of arms were a reflection of the custom adopted by noblemen where they displayed their banners outside the inn to show that they might be found within. Many public houses chose to use something to do with beer, which is where names such as The Hop Pole, The Malt and Hops (once in West Hartlepool), The Three Barrels and The Barley Mow (as in Gateshead's) originated. Gateshead also has a Brewer's Arms (later the Blue Bell), Last Orders, the Aletaster and a Malting House. York's striking gallows

sign for Ye Olde Starre Inne stretching over Stonegate is a very rare surviving example of these literally unmissable pub magnets – doing the work of a neon sign.

Royal Oak was a supporter of Charles II (he hid in one at Boscobel after the battle of Worcester in 1651 before he was king); Punch Bowl was a sign of a Whig; Marquis of Granby reflected the philanthropy of said Marquis. Chequers denoted board games while The Board proclaimed that cold meats were on offer inside – the board being what the meats were served on, hence 'board and lodge'.

In 1553 the number of pubs was restricted by law: for example, London was allowed forty, York a miserable eight and Hull a derisory three. It would be hard to find a piece of legislation that was so universally, yet happily, ignored and unenforced. In 1623 there were still 13,000 licensed premises in England. As noted Wellington's Beerhouse Act of 1830 saw licensed premises double in ten years with 25,000 new licenses issued within three months of the enactment. It also galvanised the rise and rise of the common brewery, brewing beer and selling it to outlets rather than for oneself.

Beer houses provided not just beer, but food, bar games and some even lodging. They were also known by the name 'small beer' or 'Tom and Jerry' shops. In villages and towns many shopkeepers opened their own beer shop and sold beer alongside their usual wares, just like a corner shop today. Beer would be brewed on the premises or purchased from brewers. By 1841 licences had been issue to 45,000 commercial brewers. The final remaining provisions of the Act were repealed as recently as 11 November 1993. The passing of the Act during the reign of William IV (r. 1830 – 1837) had led to numerous taverns being named in his honour; he remains 'the most popular monarch among pub names'.

When is a pub not just a pub?

Pubs were not always just pubs. Many doubled up as coroners' and magistrates' courts (the Grey Horse and the Goat in Gateshead, for example); the Queen's Head Hotel in Gateshead's Bottle Bank was very versatile as the temporary Town Hall (1867), a courthouse, a temporary home for the Roman Catholic Mission when the Catholic chapel was destroyed by fire in the 1854 Hillgate fire; it was a billiard room and a Harmony Hall (Variety Theatre); stagecoaches later had it acting as a busy posthouse. Other pubs posed as markets, morgues and as smugglers' dens (the Ship inn in Saltburn, for example); others were also blacksmith's, cobblers or carpenters – often the landlord's day job. And then there was the 'bawdy houses' – an association that goes back to Roman times. The Denmark Arms in Scarborough was also a grocers until its closure. Appropriately enough The White Boar in Huddersfield was also a butchers; fiddling the customer has always happened: in 1734 the landlord here, John Walker, was fined for giving short measures. The Beaumont Arms at Kirkheaton near Huddersfield doubled as an undertakers. The Three Nuns at Mirfield was where the nuns brewed their own ale. The Cricket Inn in Sheffield's Hyde Park had its own cricket pitch from 1826, as has The Strafford Arms at Stainborough nearby. The Victoria Park Hotel in Sheffield had a bowling green and 'an American bowling alley' in the mid-1800s. The Crooked Billet at Ryhill near Hedon housed a slaughterhouse. Scottish widow Jane McKie was a licensee at the George IV in Gateshead for over 20 years combining this with property development and her duties as an Omnibus Proprietress. Most versatile of all, though, was The Humber Tavern in Paull east of Hull; here in 1836 Trinity House decided that 'lights be exhibited in the windows of a public house at Paull as a temporary expedient until the erection of permanent lights.'

Indeed any pub that had a large enough room would accommodate local society meetings, churchwarden charity events, Freemasons and Oddfellows meetings, funeral, sickness and other benefit clubs. Gateshead's Three Tuns was where around 1891 a Jenny Hall ran the 'Women's Box' benefit club taking contributions to support women in times of illness and need. Apart from its armaments industry connotations the Old Cannon was the meeting place for medieval assize judges from Durham and the Sheriff of Northumberland to discuss serious legal matters in the two counties. Here also the wardens of St. Mary's distributed to its various charities. The Court of Justice was held for many years in the long room of the Goat, from where prisoners were sent to Durham Gaol. The Gateshead Arms opened its doors to meetings of the Association for the Prosecution of Felons. A good example of the pub as social hub is the New Cannon in Gateshead where the long room hosted all manner of local events: dinners, dances, society meetings and even travelling entertainment troupes. In the same town records for 1853 report the winners at the Crown Inn Flower and Vegetable Show and the Team Colliery Horticultural Society show at the Queen's Head (later the Victoria), both in Felling. For those who enjoyed less cerebral socialising, many pubs were venues for cockfighting; in Gateshead these included the Black Horse, Black Bull, Three Tuns (patronised by miners and quarrymen), Travellers' Rest (a beer house once called the Golden Quoit on account of its quoits pit) and the Ship. Poet Thomas Wilson mentions the Black Bull in his *The Pitman's Pay* ((1843) as a venue for 'cockfighting, cuddy racing and all other pitmen's amusements on the pay nights'. In his *Oiling of Dicky's Wig* (1926) he describes the first stagecoach trip along Low Felling's turnpike road.

Pub Entertainment: The Pub Offer

To a large extent the construction of town and village halls and other civic buildings severely curtailed the role of pubs for official business and social functions. So pubs had to do something to replace the lost takings caused by this loss; the answer lay in concerts and entertainments or 'free and easies' not dissimilar from pub open mic, pub quizzes and karaoke today.

Here is a (rather jaundiced) description of Victorian London free and easies seen through the eyes of a French visitor:

Public houses are most uncomfortable and very poorly stocked. If you go into a coffee-house, you will find only tea or coffee there, as they are not licensed to sell any other drinks. There are places one drinks without eating, others where one eats without drinking. In some oyster bars you find fish but no meat. The larger taverns are better provided with food; one can dine there, but for supper about midnight is the time when they are most popular.

The saloons are usually on the first floor of the building, and the entrance money is one shilling, in exchange for which you are given some small refreshment. The tables, covered with oil cloth or leather, are placed against the wall and partitioned off in cubicles. The Englishman likes to be isolated, he wants privacy even in public. Tea is drunk, or boiling grog, ale, inky-coloured porter or strong beer. Brandy is a favourite beverage and often served in tumblers. The room is plain, people do not go there to be amused, and drinking is a serious business. The more liquor they absorb, the quieter they become, and if occasionally a morose drinker breaks into a tipsy song, the oppressive silence soon reduces him to muteness again. This is how most Londoners who cannot afford to belong to clubs spend their evenings; and at midnight they reel homewards. Could anything be more tedious?

At the end of the room on a raised platform three gentlemen sit at a table. They are corrected dress in black swallow-tailed coats and white ties. Suddenly one of them hits the table with an auctioneer's hammer. Dead silence follows - and to the accompaniment of a piano our three gentlemen, as serious as Anglican ministers, start singing, sometimes alone, sometimes in chorus, sentimental ballads, or Anglo-Italian tunes which have the greatest success, judging by the unstinted applause they elicit. As the English have the faculty of enjoying the same thing indefinitely, this entertainment lasts for hours.

- Francis Wey, A Frenchman Sees the English in the Fifties, 1935

And:

The songs sung would not be tolerated in any reasonably regulated assembly. The comic element, as it is termed, predominates and the broader it becomes the greater favour does it obtain, any particularly bold indecency being generally received with especial applause. The meeting seldom breaks up without many of the revellers becoming the worse for drink. The "free-and-easies" are a recognized institution in the city, where the young man may take a female employee of his firm or other acquaintance, without the expense of the theatre, music-hall, or dancing academy, which would be too great a tax upon his resources. One may see young men and women in those places first introduced, who have never previously tasted drink and who listen, at first, to the questionable songs with something akin to pained surprise. Yet as others - men and women too - will laugh quite heartily, joining freely in some coarse chorus, and giving point to what is most objectionable, the new-comers will soon find their consciences dulled to the necessary level. One may hear these young women boasting of the number of glasses of wine or spirits which they can take without "Making fools of themselves."

- Tempted London, 1889

Games too became part of the pub offer. Quoits was popular with pitches and sheds in Gateshead in the Patent Hammer, the Fountain and the Plough but this lasted little more than 30 years. Billiards was introduced but this was superseded by purpose-built billiard halls. Sport too is represented with Gateshead's Cricketers Arms and the Maiden Over while Newcastle has the Clasper's Arms, after Harry Clasper (1812-1870), the famous oarsman who lived on the site of the pub at Armstrong Street and then in the pub itself. Hunting is represented by the Hound Inn (later the Lord Hill), the Fox & Hounds and the Boar's Head in Newcastle with the Talbot in Gateshead. Football boasts the Magpie and the Footballers' Arms (Footballer's Rest). Days out were very popular with pubs organising charabanc outings – in effect a motorised pub crawl as a big part of the appeal were the frequent stops at pubs on the way to the destination, and back again.

As we shall see, coaches stopped at coaching inns then 'Railway Inns' served railway passengers before and after journeys. More recently, pubs have doubled up as part-time libraries, churches and vegetable markets.

Serving the Locals

The names of pubs were often chosen to reflect the occupations and trades of their clientele. Nowhere is this more apparent than in Newcastle where we have Scottish & Newcastle patriotically stating on advertisements that 'After a good day's work for Britain – that's when beer is best'. 'Industrial' pubs include those on the Scotswood Road close to the Armstrong iron and crane works: the Forge Hammer; (later the Tyne Iron Hotel) Hydraulic Crane; the Tyne Iron and the Engineer's Arms. Armstrong's armaments trade spawned the Rifle and the Gun Hotels. In Gateshead was the Old Cannon. Other industrially named Scotswood Road hostelries (where there were 28 pubs listed in *Ward's Trade Directory* of 1911-1912) include the Vulcan Inn, the Ordnance Arms, Flax Mill Hotel (formerly the Caledonia), Shipwrights Arms, Moulders Arms (a lunchtime favourite with Vickers workers), Mechanics Arms, Blast Furnace and Ord Arms. The Hawks' Arms at 50 East Street in Gateshead remembers the Hawks family (c.1750 – 1889) - one of the most powerful British industrial dynasties of the Industrial Revolution. The Hawks owned several companies in northern England and in the City of London (including Hawks and Co., Hawks, Crawshay, and Stanley, and Hawks, Crawshay and Sons) all of which were big in iron manufacture and engineering, which they exported worldwide using their own ships. There was also a Boilermakers' Arms (Oakwellgate Chare), a Lime Kiln, a Locomotive and a (steam) Engine (Low Fell). The Brown Jug indicated a ceramics industry while the Cork Cutters' Arms was on Rabbits Bank and the Glassmakers' Arms on Pipewellgate. Newcastle's mining industry gave rise to the Colliery Engine on Shields Road and the Coal Wagon, both in Walker and the Miners Arms on the Scotswood Road. Shipbuilding too lent some names to pubs, including the Neptune after the Neptune Yard at Swan Hunters in Walker. Foremen went in the snug while workers, skilled and unskilled, drank in the bar.

On the commercial and trades front we have the Butchers' Arms in the High Street, Gateshead with Bakers'& Brewers' Arms in Newcastle's Stowell Square, the Joiners' Arms (once the Drovers' Arms), Smiths' Arms (Edward Street), Bricklayers' Arms, the Ropers Arms, and Plumbers' Arms also in Newcastle. And then there was the Three Horseshoes which was also the Horseshoe Inn in 1873. The Baxter in Hotspur Street has what is a vernacular version of baker.

In Newcastle there are many allusions to the sea, river and shipping. They include the Boathouse Inn, the Keelman, the Boat (also called the Ferry Boat Inn and the Boat House), the Steamboat Inn and the Crow's Nest. Gateshead has the Ship.

Greek mythology often crops up: in Gateshead we have the Atlas (owned by Cameron's), Hercules, the Phoenix, the Old Fleece and the Golden Fleece with a Golden Fleece on Newcastle's Scotswood Road. Roman mythology gives us the Neptune, but only indirectly (see above). Ancient British religion was represented by the Druid's Arms in Gloucester Street. The Golden Fleece shed its classical heritage when the name changed to the Pothole, famous for its first-floor balcony which resembled a theatre box.

Agricultural and horticultural names hark back to the days when what is now urban Gateshead was once rural. So, we had the Farmer's Inn in Newcastle in the Scotswood Road opposite the cattle market, the Green Tree in Laurel Street and one in Benwell, and the Foresters' Arms, while in Gateshead there was a Gardeners' Arms (previously the Free Gardeners Arms and the Oddfellows' Arms), the Plough (originally Speed the Plough), Wheatsheaf, Bee Hive, Rake and Spade (both Low Fell), and Shepherd and Shepherdess. There were three mills in Gateshead: the Windmill on Charles Street, the Old Mill on West Street, and the Five Wand Mill on Bensham Road with two Mill Inns in Newcastle's Cowgate and Westgate Road and the Millstone in Ouseburn - all indicating the ubiquity and importance of mills in pre-industrial England.

Some pubs just had attractive or curious names: examples from Newcastle include the Pine Apple (owned by Tucker's of Gateshead), Uncle Tom's Cabin (the Water Street beerhouse closed in 1874), the Picnic, the Jingling Gate (originally the Gingling Gate), Groat House, Laburnum Tree, Three Indian Kings, and the Cushy Butterfield. The pineapple is, of course, a symbol worldwide of hospitality.

'Cushy Butterfield' is a famous Geordie folk song written in the 19th century by Geordie Ridley, in the style of the music hall popular in the day. The Grace Darling, Denton Road, obviously commemorates the famous lifesaver; it was bought by Rowell's in 1897 and closed in 1924. Grace (1815 –1842) was an English lighthouse keeper's daughter. Her involvement in the rescue of survivors from the shipwrecked *Forfarshire* in 1838 brought her national fame. The paddle steamer ran aground on the Farne Islands off the coast of Northumberland; nine members of the crew were saved. The Bobby Shaftoe on Armstrong Road was originally the Alma. The Turk's Head is a common pub name, inspiring eastern exoticism but the one in Newcastle's Front Street is exceptional as it was the home of Wandering Willie – a stuffed dog. Staying in the Near East there was the Egypt Cottage on today's City Road; old OS maps reveal that places Egyptian prevailed in this area with an Egypt Court (behind the pub) and a warehouse named Egypt; indeed, the area was actually Little Egypt. No surprise then that a pub built there would have an appropriate name. The Egypt Tavern, then the Egypt Inn and finally the Egypt Cottage were thus christened.

The Beers of Choice

Up until the late 1880s the beer of choice in Newcastle was the traditional Newcastle Mild which, Lynn Pearson informs us (p. 13) was 'a strong, sweet dark ale brewed on Tyneside using poor quality local water and barley; this was the only beer available in most pubs in the 1860s but pale ales from Burton and Scotland had almost completely replaced it by 1890'. Burton brewers Bass and Allsopp stole the market and increased production of 'their clear, sparkling light ales' by the middle of the 19th century with Bass even building two new breweries in 1850 and 1865. These ales went down a treat in the north east and would have been served in pubs like the Lord Chancellor (later Maceys) in Groat Market; the Newcastle drinker was nothing if not discerning and would have appreciated the quality of Burton beers and their refreshing taste compared with local brews. The business model did not involve the usual tied houses but a system of beer agents, usually wine and spirit merchants instead who were contracted to sell beer from non-Tyneside brewers into the local trade.

Scottish beers, similarly lighter and clearer, enjoyed similar success at the same time, also using the agency method. Some of these agents were also brewers, for example W.B. Reid & Co of Newcastle's Leazes Brewery who won the William Younger of Edinburgh agency in the mid-19th century and was taken over by them in 1956. Most Scottish brewers had agencies on Tyneside by 1870; indeed 30 per cent of Younger's total output was being drunk on Tyneside by 1890 while by 1900 approximately 25 per cent of the production of Scotland's top six breweries found its way over the border to Tyneside.

Outside the Pine Apple Inn, Elswick in 1914, this group (including the local vicar) are ready to go on a trip to Wooler. The children are not impressed; and some of the blokes look rather unexcited too.

Poshing Up the Pubs

This of course led to fierce competition for the local brewers who responded by buying up the freeholds of local pubs which meant their licences were then tied to their products or those for which the brewer was an agent. Not surprisingly the tied pubs started to produce their own versions of these clear and sparkling ales. Wine and spirit merchants joined the fray to protect their agency sales leading to a significant rise in the number of pubs owned by the brewers and merchants – up to a third in some parts of Newcastle. But there was, of course, an increasing shortage of available pubs with all this frantic buying going on; the result was that, in order to draw in customers, retain market share and maintain workable margins the pub owners had to modernise their estates with curved bars, flashy mirrors and eye-catching façades. The late 19th century, then, saw a revolution in pub redesign which left us with a legacy of the many fine and opulent Victorian pubs we still see and visit to some extent in Newcastle, Gateshead and the wider area today over a century later.

In 1897 in central Newcastle there were 63 applications to modify or rebuild entirely public houses, be it from local firms or non-locals. This continued into the new century with 25 applications in 1905. Oliver & Co came late to the party when they acquired the tenancy of the Lord Chancellor in 1892 and proceeded to completely refurbish the interior.

37

Local Mergers and Consolidation

The battle of the breweries described above led to a frenetic scramble of amalgamations and takeovers. Perhaps the most significant for Newcastle was the formation of Newcastle Breweries Ltd in 1890 from four companies each with their tied houses: Newcastle's John Barras & Co Ltd and J.J. & W.H. Allison & Co; and Carr Brothers and Carr both of North Shields and Swinburne & Co of Gateshead. The result was that Newcastle Breweries Ltd could rely on over 318 pubs throughout the north east. W.B. Reid & Co was another new enterprise born of mergers in 1891 who went on to become the second biggest public house owners in 1892 with 30 houses and owning 154 in their entire sales area by the time of their takeover by William Younger in 1956. The Grainger estate was Newcastle's largest.

This concentration of brewing and pub ownership in a diminishing number of companies continued, as we all know, into the 20th century. One of the less recognised impacts of World War I was caused by wartime restrictions on transport which in turn led to a marked decline in beer consumption. Average national consumption of beer per head fell from over 30 gallons in 1900-1904 to less than 27 in 1901-1914; over investment in buying public houses did not help, nor did the rise in popularity of working men's clubs, cheap beer and unregulated opening hours. The popularity and convenience of the more family oriented leisure activities for working people – cinema, radio, sport – all disrupted the routine of 'going to the pub'. The closure of 3,736 pubs between 1906 and 1914 not surprisingly had a huge impact on beer consumption.

Beer Sign in pressed steel with Embalit paint finish reproducing advert from the former Newcastle Breweries showing a painting of the brewery.

TOON PUBS

Bacchus

Bacchus and Ariadne by Titian, in the National Gallery in London. Party time at the Bacchus

Named, of course, after the Roman god of wine, debauchery and partying. So, it's a bit of a (not unpleasant) surprise to find that it was recently refurbished with a subtle grand ocean liner theme. Its walls are now lined with black and white photos and posters that look back to Tyneside's ship building heritage: what better way to learn about the history of one of the region's greatest industries?

This is the third Newcastle incarnation of the pub. A second Bacchus stood on High Bridge from 1971 to 2001. It was demolished and rebuilt as the pub we see today. The original stood on Newgate Street from 1879 until 1971 when many old buildings were demolished to make way for the Eldon shopping centre. Going yet further back this Bass Charrington-owned pub stood on the site of an earlier cottage inn which had traded for 200 years. Men working at the Green Market nearby would call in for early morning rum and coffee. And before this it was apparently the lodgings of the jailer of the Newgate Gaol. Next door was another pub that was flattened during the same redevelopment - Bourgogne's. It was known as the Mason's Arms until around 1876 when it was bought by a firm of French winemakers called Bourgogne's. There was a modern concrete and glass version of Bourgogne's for a short while.

Bacchus 42-48 High Bridge, Newcastle upon Tyne NE1 6BX
Telephone: 0191 261 1008 • E-mail: thebacchus@sjf.co.uk
Website: https://sjf.co.uk/our-pubs/the-bacchus/

The Bee Hive

The Beehive in the black and white days with Laurel and Hardy

One of Newcastle's oldest pubs, mentioned in Newcastle's first directory of 1778 with landlord Cuthbert Burrell. It is located on the corner of the Cloth Market and High Bridge and was rebuilt in 1902 with its traditional long bar.

The ground floor exterior is attractively faced with green and yellow glazed tiles. Grade II listed, it has a bee theme inside. Above the pub are three storeys of offices, topped by an unusual ogee tower.

If you really want to know what an ogee tower is, then… 'An ogee is the name given to objects, elements, and curves—often seen in architecture and building trades—that have been variously described as serpentine-, extended S-, or sigmoid-shaped. Ogees consist of a "double curve", the combination of two semicircular curves or arcs that, as a result of a point of inflection from concave to convex or vice versa, have ends of the overall curve that point in opposite directions (and have tangents that are approximately parallel)'.

Beautiful doors

Now you know.

British Listed Buildings describes the pub as follows:

> Green and yellow ground floor has panelled and garlanded Ionic pilasters supporting entablature with leaf-bracketed frieze; original BEEHIVE HOTEL in low relief on fascia beneath prominent cornice...Pilastered angle turret has open arches under roundels and frieze; ogee dome has four very small lucarnes, with slender swept pyramidroofs, and tall spike finial.

(https://britishlistedbuildings.co.uk/101024920-beehive-hotel-westgate-ward)

After local brewer James Routledge took over in 1887 it was acquired by Newcastle Breweries in 1896, then Northern Breweries Corporation Ltd, a sister company. The green and yellow faience and the ogee tower were no accident and certainly not decoration for the sake of it. Both features were designed to make the pub stand out from a distance amongst the less exciting shops and offices adjacent on Cloth Market and High Bridge; both shouted out 'this is a pub! Come on in'.

The remarkable green and yellow faience

The Beehive, *2 High Bridge, Newcastle upon Tyne NE1 1EN Telephone: 0191 232 5017*

The Black Garter

The Black Garter pub is at Newcastle's historic Grainger Market. In *Heady days - A History of Newcastle Public Houses (Vol 1 the Central Area)* by Brian Bennison he explains how two Bass pubs, the Star & Garter and the Black Swan were merged, and a sweet shop was swallowed up. The new establishment was somewhat boringly named the Market Tavern but later, in an outbreak of linguistic gymnastics, it became the much more exciting Black Garter.

The Black Garter

The Black Garter, 31 Clayton Street, Newcastle upon Tyne NE1 5PN
Telephone: 0191 260 2099 • E-mail: blackgarter.newcastle@stonegatepubs.co.uk

The Bodega

ASir John Fitzgerald pub famous for its traditional long bar, Victorian stained-glass domes, elaborately tiled floors, and its history. Formerly the Black Bull until 1995, according to Whatpub.com: 'Two fine stained glass domes are the architectural highlights of the pub… with separate booths for more intimate drinking. A number of old brewery mirrors adorn the walls'.

New research suggests that the Bodega could be the oldest in Newcastle, reaching as far back as 1441. Local archaeology company AAG has revealed that the Bodega may be the latest incarnation of an ale house that has stood on the site since medieval times. So, not only could the pub be the oldest in Newcastle, it could also be one of the top ten oldest pubs in the country.

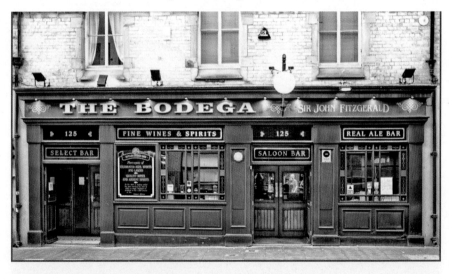

AAG archaeologist Jon Welsh said: "There seems to be a common misconception or urban myth that the pub was once a mosque, due to the large open bar and the domed windows at the back of the bar." The current building is an 1872 rebuild of an earlier pub, the first of its domes being built in 1906, the second dome added in 1937.

"Westgate Road is part of an ancient route crossing the country through a gap in the Pennines made by the River Tyne. It was used by the Romans and probably ancient Britons before them. Even today Westgate Road is the only

medieval radial road that still reaches into the heart of the city. The Bodega has benefitted from being on such an important route by being part of its long and varied history".

There was a pub here called the Nevyll Inne or Neville Inn as early as 1441 in an ideal location for an inn or tavern. *"Wherever the Neville Inn was, it was probably pulled down in 1644 to prevent the approaching Parliamentarian forces using it for cover during the siege of the town that marked the Civil War in the North."*

"The Old George in the Cloth Market was built in the sixteenth century, but only one window and a chimney breast survive from the original building. Most of what remains was built in the eighteenth and nineteenth centuries."

Down the decades the Bodega's colourful history has seen it supplied by its own brewery, provide refreshment for the mob at several public executions, it has housed a barbershop and tenement flats under its roof, been a forerunner in the long bar revolution, and played host to the city's early gay scene.

During the 1970s when the Westgate Road was home to pornographic cinemas and adult bookshops, the pub was a venue for strippers performing underneath the rear dome.

The Bodega's assistant manager John Ritchie said: *"Certainly, back in the day, the pub had a reputation as a house of ill-repute, with gambling and rumours of a brothel. Hopefully it's a bit different these days!"*

The Bodega, 125 Westgate Rd, Newcastle upon Tyne NE1 4AG
Telephone: 0191 2211552 • Website: https://sjf.co.uk/our-pubs/the-bodega/

The Bridge Tavern,
Quayside

*The Bridge today: who can tell what treasures
await you inside?'*

Formerly (or still according to the façade) the Newcastle Arms. Situated right under Newcastle-Gateshead's Tyne Bridge; there has been a hostelry and ale House on this site for nearly two centuries with the original building demolished in 1925 to make way for the new bridge. The new pub was built during the construction of the bridge: you can see the bridge supports on either side of the pub. A fully operational in-house microbrewery has been installed in association with Wylam Brewery.

Original, and tasteful features include several original green Bauhaus lamps hanging from the ceiling above a central table.

The walls are lined with books leading to 'Keith's corner', an area complete with large tables and the books of Newcastle jazz legend Keith Crombie who died in 2012. They were bequeathed to the pub, not for sale, but for reading over a over a pint. Heaven.

The microbrewery

The lights

That wonderful library

On 28 June 2012, a powerful lightning bolt struck the Tyne Bridge. Being dark, it lit up the roads all around. The bolt, part of a super-cell thunderstorm, came with heavy rain – a month's worth of rainfall in just two hours – causing flash flooding on Tyneside.

The bridge and nearby structures are used as a nesting site by a colony of around 700 pairs of black-legged kittiwakes, the furthest colony inland in the world.

The seven world famous bridges across the Tyne, which link the city to Gateshead on the south bank of the river are from west to east: the Redheugh Bridge, King Edward VII Bridge, Queen Elizabeth II Bridge, The High Level Bridge, the Swing Bridge, the George V Bridge (or Tyne Bridge) and the Gateshead Millennium Bridge.

◄— *Inside the Bridge*
Under the bridge, from the yard

The Bridge Tavern, 7 Akenside Hill, Newcastle upon Tyne, NE1 3UF
Telephone: 0191 261 9966 • E-mail: bridgetavern@vaulkhardgroup.co.uk

The Broad Chare

First off, let's deal with that name. Just as in York, bars are actually gates, so in Newcastle chares are streets or lanes. Numerous medieval jetties were a significant feature of the Quayside where the river between the wooden jetties was gradually filled in with rubble. Houses were subsequently built on the land that this created and the old wooden jetties evolved into narrow riverside alleys called 'chares'. Chare is an Anglo-Saxon word meaning, 'a ninety degree turn' or bend (like a chair) and such alleys often projected from neighbouring streets at this angle. After the great fire of Newcastle and Gateshead in 1854, a number of the chares were permanently removed although some still remain today. [https://englandsnortheast.co.uk/newcastle-quayside/].

Most of the chares descend down to the Tyne. A map of 1736 shows twenty chares along the Quayside from Sandhill in the west to the end of the town wall at Sandgate in the east although other lanes and alleyways called chares could be found around the town, away from the river. Unsurprisingly, Broad Chare is thus named because it was (untypically of chares), broad and wide enough for a cart.

'Broad Chare' courtesy
© Trudy Kepke and
www.artthroughalens.co.uk

'The Broad Chare' pub occupies part of a former theatre box office (although some say 'housed within a converted warehouse by the quay'); it is a traditional Victorian red-brick building redolent of Newcastle's industrial heritage.

This traditional city pub is housed over two floors, the ground floor is where you can have a quiet drink or bar snack, while the full menu is available upstairs in the dining room, with its stripped wood floors, leather banquettes set against simply laid solid wood tables and chairs. House ales are supplied by Wylam Brewery including their own-label brew, 'The Writers Block' – essential drinking during research for book writing.

Inside the Broad Chare

Broad Chare, *Quayside, Newcastle Upon Tyne, Tyne and Wear, NE1 3DQ
Telephone: 0191 211 2144
Website: https://thebroadchare.co.uk/*

MIDDLEWHITE PORK CRACKLING 4.50
w/ BRAMLEY APPLE SAUCE
LANCASHIRE CHEESE CROQUETTES 4.50
SCOTCH EGG 6.50
MONKFISH CHEEKS w/ TARTARE SAUCE 6.50
CRISPY PIGS EARS 5
1/4 PINT PRAWNS IN THE SHELL 6
HAND RAISED PORK PIE w/ PICCALILLI 6.50
CAULIFLOWER FRITTERS w/CURRY MAYO 5.50
LINDISFARNE OYSTERS 3.50 EACH

Eclectic bar menu to say the least

'Everytime I walk along the beautiful Quayside in Newcastle I always love looking at this old building. The curves are wonderful and stand proud amongst all the other old buildings that Newcastle has to offer. Overlooking the River Tyne and The Sage and also the Millennium Bridge, this is a very iconic old building that I loved making into one of my rainy colourful scenes'.

- https://artthroughalens.co.uk/streetscenes/p/broad-chare-newcastle-quayside. Trudy Kepke, artist

'The eleventh creative commission set to us by top chef-restaurateur Terry Laybourne, to design The Broad Chare pub and restaurant just off Newcastle's Quayside. The brief was to re-define what a 'proper pub' should be like in the 21st century. Our approach was to identify iconic aspects of the great British pub then express them in a contemporary, yet familiar, fashion. We paired traditional stripped wooden floors and painted brickwork with deep rich colours and tactile textures; and contrasted frosted glass partitions with bar tops made from beautiful reclaimed oak pews. All creating an inviting bar and restaurant environment which quickly proved a success with customers'.

- https://www.wardrobinsondesign.com/story/

'A collaboration between local luminary Terry Laybourne's 21 Hospitality Group and [the adjoining] Live Theatre, a new writing theatre based nearby, this proper old-school ale-house isn't aiming for the skies, but it does what it does – well-kept beer and bar food – very well indeed; a further boon – "the new outdoor terrace makes it even better!"'.

- https://www.hardens.com/az/restaurants/newcastle-upon-tyne/ne1/the-broad-chare.htm

Other chares include Pudding Chare, Grinding / Grindon / Granden / Grundon Chare, Blue/Blew Anchor Share,Pepper Corn Chare, Palester's / Black Boy Chare , Colwins / Colevin's / Colvin's (Armourer's) Chare, Hornsby's Chare (formerly Maryon House Chare), Plumber / Plummer Chare — "Cyprian nymphs dwelled here". "Robert Plumber, bailiff, 1376", "Plomer chare" (Beverley chaire). "John Plummer, coal merchant", Fenwick's Entry / Kirk Chare,The Park / Back Lane / Dark Chare / Blind Chare , Peacock's Chare — from the inn which took its name. The inn moved to Trinity Chare; Trinity Chare (Dalton Place) at Three Indian Kings Court/Hotel, leads to Broad Chare. Rewcastle / Rucastle Chare. Byker / Baker Chare — named after Robert de Byker; Cock's / Coxton's / Cox / Cockis Chare (Ratten Row). Likely named after Ralph Cock, alderman and mayor, 1653. Love Lane (Gowerley's Rawe/Gowlar Row/Gowelery Chare) — foot of the Wall Knoll. Birthplace of Lord Eldon and Lord Stowell. [Prodigious research by Caroline Hagan; see https://blueocto.medium.com/the-chares-of-newcastle-city-254bdff2daf5 for many more chares].

Centurion Bar

This truly opulent room was built in 1893 as a sumptuous waiting lounge for first-class rail passengers, a highlight being its exquisite tiling which was valued at £3.8 million in 2001. The lounge and its bar closed in the 1960's when the British Transport Police began using it as cells. As if that wasn't sacrilege enough, an unthinkable act of idiotic cultural vandalism occurred when the dullards at British Rail, who then owned it, glossed over the building's Grade 1 listed status and, according to the *Chronicle*, 'took sledge hammers to some of the walls, putting in external piping and painting the tiles a lurid red; a bit like The Louvre slapping a fresh coat of paint over The Monet [sic] Lisa'.

https://www.chroniclelive.co.uk/special-features/once-upon-time-beautiful-bar-13722575

The paper in 2017 goes on to tell how

'In 2000, Keeping Inn Ltd acquired the building and lovingly and painstakingly restored The Centurion to its former glory. Since opening, the grandeur of the John Dobson designed interior has been enjoyed by thousands of customers, both visitors, locals and regulars to Newcastle upon Tyne. There are no strangers at the Centurion Bar, only friends you haven't yet met'.

-www.northumbria.info adds

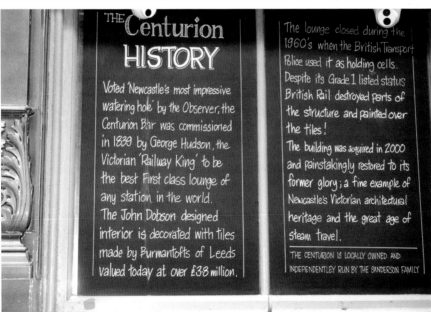

THE Centurion
HISTORY

Voted 'Newcastle's most impressive watering hole' by the Observer, the Centurion Bar was commissioned in 1839 by George Hudson, the Victorian 'Railway King' to be the best First class lounge of any station in the world.
The John Dobson designed interior is decorated with tiles made by Burmantofts of Leeds valued today at over £38 million.

The lounge closed during the 1960's when the British Transport Police used it as holding cells. Despite its Grade 1 listed status British Rail destroyed parts of the structure and painted over the tiles!
The building was acquired in 2000 and painstakingly restored to its former glory; a fine example of Newcastle's Victorian architectural heritage and the great age of steam travel.

THE CENTURION IS LOCALLY OWNED AND INDEPENDENTLEY RUN BY THE SANDERSON FAMILY

As part of an 1892 scheme by North East Railway architect Willian Bell the waiting room from John Dobson's Central Station was clad in fabulous tiling to emerge as the First Class Refreshment Room. It is decorated from floor to high ceiling in Burmantofts Baroque style top-lit by a tile clad skylight, with columns dominating both ends of the room. A 14 ft square mural by Byron Dawson takes pride of place between two 20 ft high Doric obelisks. Burmantofts, of Leeds, was the best known producer of tiles and architectural ceramics until the firm closed down in the late 1950's. Another great example of Burmantofts tiles in Newcastle is the Central Arcade.

Some of this text is taken from an article by Alastair Gilmour for the *Newcastle Journal*.

Centurion Bar, *Grand Central Station, Neville Street, Newcastle NE1 5DG*
Telephone: 0191 261 6611 • www.centurion-newcastle.com
Facebook: www.facebook.com/centurionbar

City Tavern

The tavern was originally established in 1923 with its mock-Tudor façade but the iconic Newcastle building was built in 1872 as stables cum livery. It has since undergone many incarnations including office accommodation, a garage (Adams 1918-1922). In 1923 the front elevation was remodelled and that's when the famous façade went up. From that time it was operated by a local company 'Carrick's Dairy Ltd.' (1925-1951), followed by a restaurant named Cottage Restaurant (1951-1959), then as the well-known Carrick's Café (1959-1962). The premises remained as a café- restaurant between 1962 and 1971 under the ownership of Carrick's and was called Tilley's Café.

Inside and outside the City Tavern today - https://www.citytavern.co.uk/gallery/

'In 2018 we approached the much acclaimed Wylam Brewery to create a house beer for us. The result was Alfie Blonde, a single malt hoppy blonde ale sitting at 4.2%. Triple hopped for a lovely extra thump of grapefruit and sherbet lemon. Being hoppy with a slight bitterness to it means it goes down perfectly with a classic fish and chips, of which we do the best in the 'toon''.

In 1971 the property became one of Newcastle's most famous pubs. In spring 2014 LYH was refurbished and re-opened under its original name, City Tavern and 'was transformed into the city's most sumptuous venue providing laid back comfort, good food, good ales, and good friends'.

https://www.citytavern.co.uk/about-us/ethos/

City Tavern, *10 Northumberland Road, Newcastle Upon Tyne, NE1 8JF*
Telephone: 0191 232 1308 • E-mail: hello@citytavern.co.uk

The Cluny

The Cluny has been staging bands from across the globe since 1999. According to Helen Gildersleeve* the Cluny, once the home of a bottling plant, 'is now a post-industrial bar with separate music rooms that thinks like a pub and doesn't try to be something it isn't'. You want an affordable, decent band night with a variety of beers and tasty pub grub (they even do chips and gravy in a baguette)? Look no further. 'Music and beer is the Cluny's USP and the reason behind its popularity across the region…'

'The Cluny's raison d'être is music – from the moment you step inside the industrial brick walls are adorned with posters advertising forthcoming bands from The Monkey Junk Blues Club to Reverend Peyton's Big Damn Band and a 20-year anniversary celebration of Radiohead's OK Computer, where fans and musicians come together to perform. It hosts over 400 gigs a year, all of which are well attended… Notable acts that have graced its stages include Mumford & Sons, Arctic Monkeys, Seasick Steve, The Futureheads and Duffy'.

It occupies a former flax spinning mill which opened in 1848. It then re-opened as a steam powered flour mill in 1860 before taking its namesake from when it became a whisky bottling plant decades later.

- *'From Whiskey and Flour to an Unbeatable Music Hub', August 11, 2017

The Cluny, 36 Lime St., Ouseburn, Newcastle Upon Tyne, Tyne & Wear, NE1 2PQ
Telephone: 0191 230 4474 • E-mail: info@thecluny.com

The Crown Posada
Quayside

A historic pub interior of regional importance, CAMRA

This delightful Grade II listed building boasts two beautiful stained glass windows designed by George Joseph Baguley and manufactured by William Wailes, whose private residence was Saltwell Towers in Gateshead. The 230-year-old pub was rebuilt in 1880 and apparently was bought by a Spanish sea captain for his mistress. The sailor, who had made his fortune in India, was married to a woman in Spain but also kept a mistress in Newcastle who ended up joining him at the pub.

Inside the Crown Posada

Originally known as The Crown, the Spanish word 'posada' for inn or resting place, was added later. In 2020 it was designated by the city council as an Asset of Community Value which allows local community groups the right to put forward a plan to take it over, if it is ever sold.

In 2015 staff discovered four Spanish silhouette murals behind wallpaper featuring scenes of a flamenco dancer and a civil war re-enactment. The red and black-painted murals, by what has usually been thought an unknown artist [but see below] and said to date back to 1903, were discovered during an earlier refurbishment about 15 years ago but, astonishingly, went unreported. Sadly, the *Chronicle* tells us 'the mural has been preserved using specialist techniques and is already out of sight once more, hidden by a protective decorative wall covering. So, the mystery Spanish scenes will not be available to view again - until the next refurbishment'. [https://www.chroniclelive.co.uk/news/north-east-news/historic-newcastle-pub-crown-posada-10367142] 2015.

The 75 -year-old mystery has finally been solved, as Alastair Gilmour uncovers:

The year was 1947… the murals now hidden behind the wallpaper in the Crown Posada were getting sketched out in charcoal by three 17-year-old Gosforth Grammar School pupils, Mike Attewell, Tristram Storey and Douglas Wood.

Seventy-five years later, Mike Attewell's daughter Helen breezed into the iconic

The elusive murals

pub earlier this year with a copy of Cheers North East – dated November 2015 – which featured the artworks blinking briefly in the sunlight for the few hours they had between the removal of the old wallpaper and its replacement during a refurbishment.

"My dad did those," she said to manager Andrew Nicholson, who has spent most of the past decade researching the history of the pub... The story of the murals had previously been left to educated guesswork and conjecture. "I thought the paintings' history was lost to time until I met Helen," says Andrew. "She nonchalantly told me her father had done the paintings and more than that he was alive and well and living in Durham. After I picked my jaw up off the bar I got as many details as I could over a pint."

Theories had abounded over the provenance of the Spanish dancer, bullfighter, guitar players and donkey rider depicted so beautifully on the painted plaster. Were they in homage to a former owner's Spanish mistress? Did they have something to do with the Spanish embassy that operated further up Dean

The beautiful windows: mistress and sea captain

Street? Do they contain a hidden message?

We'll let Mike Attewell take up the story:

"Three young students were idle between school and college. Their old art teacher, Charles Fallows, told them of a potential job decorating a pub with murals... "Naturally the theme for Crown & Posada (as Mike recalls it was named then) was Spanish. Less naturally, the colours were yellow, orange and red – their impact, thank goodness, a little lessened by using an appearance of stencilling. A life-size fighting-bull plunged across the bar room wall, its horns level with the pints. On another wall, a flamenco dancer flared her skirt while her partner stamped his heels – and turned to applaud his own backside in the usual style.

"Elsewhere there was a landscape which had to be genuine, though it was out of date because it was copied from an El Greco painting, and there was a figure of a peasant with a donkey, who might have been Sancho Pansa. All this we never saw again – being good students we never went into pubs, although we did allow the exception of the Union bar, where the beer was cheaper.

"We were paid £25 between us, without hearing any criticism or praise that I remember. Inevitably the murals were papered over, being integral with the rest of the interior. Whether that happened years later or the following month, I cannot say."

Apart from the fine beer, great crack and enthusiastic welcome, the Crown Posada is also noted for its huge mirrors and two stained glass windows designed by George Joseph Baguley and manufactured by William Wailes, whose private residence was Saltwell Towers in Gateshead.

It's also worth looking at the ceiling's deeply recessed panels and frames with their guilloche and egg-and-dart ornament. Until a 2004 refurbishment, they were picked out in amazing reds, golds and greens, but were subsequently whitewashed into history.

- *Source: Alastair Gilmour, Cheers North East*

CAMRA tells us

'The long, narrow interior has a high ornate moulded ceiling with deeply recessed panels. Front left is a delightful, small, screened-off snug with impressive Pre-Raphaelite-style stained-glass windows depicting a lady serving a drink and a Tudor gent about to consume it. Drinks can be ordered from

the side of the servery, but this was once covered by a curtain with service via a tiny hinged stained-glass window attached to the bar-back. The bar fittings are primarily original albeit with some modern replacements e.g. the mirrors and stained-glass panels on top of the four-bay bar-back. The two side panels separating the front public bar from the rear sitting room survive and have colourful leaded pictorial panels at the top (but the door has gone)... The gents' has a terrazzo floor and the doors to both the ladies' and gents' are of an inter-war style and, again, could date from the early 1950s. Music comes from a 1941 turntable record player situated on the bar counter and customers are encouraged to bring their vinyl LP's to play.'

We learn from the John Fitgerald website:

The Crown Posada is part of the Sir John Fitzgerald (SJF) group; Fitzgerald was born in Tipperary in 1857. After completing an apprenticeship in the wine and spirit trade, he moved to Newcastle in 1878 and set up his own business. In 1896, he branched out and bought his first licensed premises, becoming a pioneer of the long bar system which would revolutionise social drinking in England. By 1900 John Fitzgerald owned bars across the North East and also began manufacturing aerated water and bottling ales in a plant adjoining his headquarters in Pilgrim Street.

In 2020 the Sir John Fitzgerald group was acquired in a multimillion-pound deal by Ladhar Group for an undisclosed amount in a deal which ensures the company's North East heritage and ownership remain firmly in the city.

The Ladhar Group has a leisure portfolio, which includes the likes of Pleased To Meet You, Red House, Lady Grey's and the Gunner Tavern in Newcastle and will now add 16 sites to its growing portfolio, including Crown Posada, The Bodega and The Bacchus, as well as sites in Stockton, North Tyneside, Gateshead and Northumberland.

- [https://sjf.co.uk/our-story/]

***The Crown Posada**, 31 Side, Newcastle upon Tyne NE1 3JE*
Telephone: (0191) 232 1269 • Website http://sjf.co.uk/our-pubs/crown-posada/

The Crow's Nest

The current building near Haymarket is dated 1902 and was a hotel; there was an earlier Crow's Nest on the street in the early-mid 19th century, or possibly earlier. In the 1980s and 1990s it went by the silly names Inventions and Bar Oz but has now, thankfully, reverted to its original name. The first and second floor rooms contain elaborate plasterwork decoration. On the second floor there is a large panelled ballroom with a decorated plaster vault.

When the original pub was built it was surrounded by trees in which a colony of nesting rooks nested and gave the pub its name. Unfortunately many of the trees were cut down in the 1860's and the rooks moved on. The original Crows Nest pub had looked like a country cottage with a red tiled roof.

The old Crow's Nest

The current Crow's Nest

The present Crows Nest was acquired by Newcastle Breweries in 1896 and further remodelled in 1899 and 1902. The Crows Nest closed in the 1960's and had the nickname "Feathers and Twigs". During its golden years, this was one of Newcastle Breweries "flagship" hostelries and it has some "luxurious" features. Was, and maybe still is, one of the few places you can get Stu Brew beers, brewed by the students at Newcastle University just behind the building. It is Europe's first student-run microbrewery.

The Crow's Nest, *137 Percy Street, Newcastle upon Tyne NE1 7RY*
Telephone(0191) 261 2607 • E-mail: 7179@greeneking.co.uk
Website greeneking-pubs.co.uk/pubs/tyne-and-wear...

The Cumberland Arms

A historic pub interior of regional importance
https://pubheritage.camra.org.uk/pubs/160

The Cumberland Arms first opened in 1898, 'a unique pub which is frequently bursting at the seams with folk musicians, spoken word events and comedy gigs'.

The first edition of the *Ordnance Survey* map of the lower Ouseburn Valley, surveyed in 1859 and published in 1861 shows at least 38 public houses, although the Cumberland Arms isn't one of them. It is simply shown on the map as one of the dwellings that formed Byker Buildings, and it wasn't until 1862 that it was first licensed as a beer house.

Thankfully, since its rebuilding in 1898-9 by James T. Cackett, it hasn't changed much; it was one of several owned, according to a plaque outside, by John ('Jocker') Wood, a well-known local sportsman and publican. At the central entrance the old off-sales hatch remains. On the left is the public bar which retains its original counter, mirrored bar-back and full-height match-board panelled walls and ceiling. One interesting feature is the fine bar-back and counter, which were moved to the Cumberland from the Haymarket Hotel, Percy Street when the latter was demolished in 1987.

The 1871 census reveals that the Cumberland started life as a dwelling - No. 30 Byker Buildings.* The website [https://www.thecumberlandarms.co.uk/history/] tells us that it was occupied by John Lightfoot, a mill furnace-man, his wife and child. Soon after, he was able to become an innkeeper through the Beer House Act 1830 permitting any rate-payer to sell beer in a bid to deter people from strong spirits. Lightfoot was selling wine by 1889 and was granted a music and singing licence two years later. And so began the Cumberland's enduring tradition of music and the performing arts.

The Cumberland Arms was a true industrial workers' pub, surrounded as it was by two lead works, glass, canvas and iron works, two potteries, a sweet

The interior with that splendid back bar and window.

factory and the cattle sanatorium. Then there was the Cluny whisky warehouse near City Farm, a former lead works. In 1896 close by the Byker Bank crossing of the Ouse Burn here were eleven pubs.

The website continues: No 28 was swallowed up and the Cumberland Arms was sold in 1897 boasting a bar, tap room, bagatelle room, cellar and four living rooms. In 1898 plans were drawn up by Benjamin Simpson for a more elaborate building which included a tower on the north-west corner. According to the newsletter of the Ouseburn Trust Heritage Group Spring 2008, despite the plans receiving approval from the Council, the owner, a Mr Thompson of Whickham, rejected the idea and instead engaged James Cackett to make some internal alterations and build a new façade. It was while making the alterations to the pub that the front of the pub collapsed, unfortunately resulting in the death by falling debris, of one of the workmen, Matthew Fitzgerald. Ironically, this was an event which later saved the Cumberland.

The Chartist, William Parker, 'an outspoken critic of class inequality' is celebrated here with this wall plaque.

'On Friday 13 August 2021 the Lord Mayor of Newcastle, Councillor Habib Rahman unveiled a blue plaque to William Parker; Labourer, Chelsea pensioner and leading Newcastle Chartist. The plaque is situated at the Cumberland Arms on James Street, the site of the Byker Buildings where the Ouseburn Charter Association used to meet in 1840-42. Parker was self educated, not only learning to read and write, but to display in his writings a wide reading and grasp of history'.

- https://nelh.net/blue-plaque-unveiled-to-william-parker-ouseburn-chartist/

From 1908 the pub was one of three owned by John "Jocker" Wood (1854-1937), the others being the Masons Arms on Quality Row and the Duke of York on Back Maling Street. Jocker Wood was a renowned quoits player establishing his famous quoits Handicap Tournament there. The Cumberland had its own quoits yard. Jocker was also a keen professional runner and rower, and was a successful pigeon breeder.

Newcastle Chartists

William Parker
1790 - 1858

Labourer, Chelsea Pensioner, and Chartist. An outspoken critic of class inequality. Lived at Lime Street 1838-58. Chairman of the Ouseburn Charter Association, which met in a school room at Byker Buildings 1840-42.

City of Newcastle upon Tyne

Now, in an average year, the pub puts on over 900 artists, hosts more than 90 community events, 180 performances and 150 dance rehearsals in addition to over 350 back-room sessions. 2022 saw their birthday celebrations over a fortnight from early August.

* "Stories of the Cumberland Arms, Byker"©, podcasts, transcripts, history timeline and other information.

Cumberland Arms, *James Place Street, off Byker Bank, Newcastle upon Tyne, Tyne and Wear, NE6 1LD • Telephone: 0191 265 6151*
E-mail: info@thecumberlandarms.co.uk

The Dog & Parrot

The Dog & Parrot is near Newcastle Central Station and next to Times Square. It's famous for the now iconic murals of music's legendary superheroes including David Bowie, Prince and Aretha Franklin - worth a visit alone. Originally a Whitbread & Co. Ltd homebrew house founded December 1982 on a malt-extract plant. Ceased brewing 1989.

By May 1995 it was called The Tut and Shive, before later reverting to The Dog and Parrott.

The Dog & Parrot, *52 Clayton Street West, Newcastle upon Tyne, NE1 4EX*
Telephone: 0191 261 6998 • E-mail: hello@thedogandparrot.co.uk

---

Fitzgeralds

In common with the Crown Posada and the Bridge Hotel, Fitzgeralds is a Sir John Fitzgerald pub, although you probably worked that out from the name. 'The beer is canny'.

Fitzgeralds, *60 Grey Street, Newcastle upon Tyne, NE1 6AF*
Telephone: (0191) 230 1350 • Website sjf.co.uk/our-pubs/fitzgeralds-newcastle...

The Five Swans

Formerly Luckies. Wetherspoon tells us that it is 'A Grade II listed building, officially opened by King Olav V of Norway in 1968. The central lawn in the Quadrangle is open to the public and contains a fine bronze sculpture by David Wynne of Swans in Flight. The Five Swans rising from the pool of water 'reflect the city's long-established links with Scandinavia'. The five countries (Denmark, Sweden, Finland, Norway and Iceland) are each represented by a wild swan'.

The walls of this interesting pub are decorated with photos and descriptions of some of Newcastle's most famous sons (no daughters!), iconic places and products making it a virtual mini local encyclopaedia. Here are just a few of them taken from the text under the photographs:

Sir Charles Algernon Parsons

'Following his graduation from Cambridge, with a first in mathematics, he joined W.G. Armstrong as an apprentice engineer in Newcastle. In 1884 he gained a senior position with Newcastle ship engine manufacturers, Clarke, Chapman & Co.

In his first year with the firm, he revolutionised the maritime industry forever. He developed a turbine engine that drove an electrical generator, which he had also designed. The result was a steam turbine that made cheap and plentiful electricity possible.

In 1889, he founded C.A. Parsons and Co. in Newcastle to produce turbo-generators to his design. Over the next few years, improvement in efficiency led to the first megawatt turbine in 1899. His ground breaking technology was fitted into some of Britain's most prestigious battleships and transatlantic liners'

Paddy's Market

'There are records of a market being held on the quayside at Newcastle from as early as 1717. Daily markets were held for selling fish, herbs, bread, cloth and leather, but on Saturdays, the milk market was home to Paddy's market where old clothes were laid out on straw and on the walls of the old town. The practice continues into the latter half of the 20th century and people today can still recall being told to tidy their room because it looked like 'Paddy's market'.'

Swan Hunter

'Swan Hunter was founded by George Burton Hunter and the widow of Charles Sheridan Swan in 1880. In 1903, it merged with Wigham Richardson in an attempt to secure the prestigious contract of building *RMS Mauretania*. The bid was successful, and the new company based in Wallsend, went on to construct the largest and fastest ship in the world. *The Mauretania* was launched from Wallsend on September 20, 1906 by the Duchess of Roxburghe. The Cunard express liner captured the Blue Riband for the fastest transatlantic crossing in 1907, and held the record for twenty-two years.

Another famous ship built at the Tyneside shipyard was the *RMS Carpathia* which rescued the survivors from the *RMS Titanic* in 1912. She was transporting American troops to Europe during the First World War when she was torpedoed and sunk on 17 July 1918 by a German U-boat. During a 130 year existence, Swan Hunter built over 1,600 vessels, including 100 warships for the Royal Navy, as well as the flagship, *HMS Ark Royal,* which was launched in 1985.

By 2007 with no fresh orders and competition from the Far East, ship production at the historic site finally ceased'.

Newcastle Brown Ale

Full details are in the Breweries chapter under Scottish & Newcastle.

Ringtons Tea

Began in 1907, when Samuel Smith moved from Leeds to Newcastle to set up his own tea delivery business. He secured an investment of £250 from his business partner William Titte*rington*. The name 'Ringtons' is derived from the latter part of his surname. With an 'S' added from the Smith.

Sam began making door to door tea delivered in his famous horse and carriage. The business began to grow, and by the following year Sam was employing four people and two horses. In the early 1920s, Ringtons began using cars, but most customers preferred their tea delivered in the traditional manner, and it wasn't until 1962 that the last horse retired.

By the Second World War, Ringtons had over 400 employees...After more than 100 years, Ringtons continue their door-to-door service, delivering to over 270,000 households.

Vilyam Fisher

'Fisher was born in 1903 in Clara Street, Newcastle. His parents were exiled German-Russians and his father, a committed Bolshevik, continued to conduct gun smuggling operations from his new home in the North East. The family soon moved to Whitley Bay, where Vilyam was schooled. He later apprenticed as a draughtsman at Swan Hunter, Wallsend, before enrolling at London University in 1920.

He returned to the Soviet Union after his studies and worked as a translator. He was employed as a radio operator during his military service of 1925, and was subsequently recruited in this role by the Russian secret police. After a decade of international field work, he returned to Russia to train future operatives in the clandestine skills he had perfected.

Fisher entered the United States as a spy in 1947 and as a cover for his illegal residence, opened an artist's studio in Brooklyn. He made no attempt to sell paintings, but continued working on his technique, to give greater credence to his elaborately constructed alias.

Fisher was captured by the FBI on June 21, 1957. Upon his arrest he gave the name Rudolf Abel, which was a code name tell the Russians that he has been caught. He was sentenced to thirty years in prison, but in 1962, was exchanged for the CIA U-2 pilot Gary Powers and an American student Frederic Pryor. After his return to Moscow he continued his intelligence work for the KGB and was rewarded for his service with the Order of Lenin.

Mark Freuder Knopfler OBE

Born in Glasgow in 1949... having settled in his mother's hometown of Blyth by the age of seven, Mark was inspired by his uncle Kingsley's harmonica and boogie-woogie piano-playing. He graduated from Leeds University with a degree in English and worked as a journalist and part-time lecturer while also

playing in various bands in Leeds, London and Newcastle. In 1977, he formed Dire Straits with his brother David and recorded their first demos including 'Sultans of Swing' and 'Down To The Waterline', which recalled Mark's life in Newcastle.

Andrews Liver Salts

First marketed in 1894…the name 'Andrews' was chosen because the company offices were situated close to St Andrew's Church, in Newgate Street, Newcastle. The 4oz and 8oz tins were exported all over the world as a pleasant tasting tonic relief, for symptoms caused by over-indulgence the night before.

Hank Marvin

Born Brian Robson Rankin on 28 October 1941 in Newcastle upon Tyne. He played the banjo and piano as a child, until he heard Buddy Holly, and decided that he wanted to be a guitarist. The name Hank Marvin… is a combination of his childhood nickname of Hank, and a country and western signer he admired named Marvin Rainwater.

When Marvin was sixteen he met Johnny Foster, Cliff Richard's manager, at a coffee bar in Soho, London. Foster was looking for a guitarist to play in Richard's backing band, The Drifters. Marvin accepted the position providing the band could also accommodate his friend Bruce Welch. The Drifters became The Shadows in early 1959 to avoid confusion with the American R&B group. They featured under their new name for the first time on Richard's sixth single 'Travellin' Light'. Cliff Richard and the Shadows dominated British pop music in the late 1950s and early 1960s, leading John Lennon to later claim that "before Cliff and the Shadows, there has been nothing worth listening to in British music."'

Swans in Flight by David Wynne at Newcastle Civic Centre, Newcastle. 21 May 2018, photographer is Christopher Down

The Five Swans, *14 St Mary's Pl, Newcastle upon Tyne NE1 7PG Telephone: 0191 211 1140*

The Forth,
Pink Lane

Previously famous for hosting Victorian boxing matches, it was once run by Canadian born Tommy Burns (originally Noah Brusso), a former world heavyweight boxing champion. Tommy reigned from 1906-08, before going on to run the pub from 1921-27. He held illegal fist fights in an upstairs room and squared up to a policeman in a raid when he was investigated for serving after- hours drinks. On leaving England he ran a speakeasy in New York during the prohibition years. Nowadays local art decorates the walls.

The Forth is steeped in history, named as it was after the public space in which it stood. Here are some 19th century accounts of its long journey to the

Forth with stunning art decorating the walls from local international artist Hush and Bobzilla, mural artist and illustrator. See wellhung.co.uk and bobzilla.co.uk

21st century; it is the sad story of 'the decline and loss of what was once the nicest place in Newcastle' from Volume 1 of the *Monthly Chronicle of North Country Lore and Legend* published in June 1887:

Nowhere else in Newcastle 'has excited more interest among the inhabitants than the open space called the Forth. It was for ages a playground for old and young; there the children used to bowl their eggs at Easter; and there Ned Corvan's songs was a lamentation for the loss of the Forth. The very site of it is now but dimly remembered, even by the oldest inhabitants of Newcastle'. *Mackenzie's History of Newcastle* condenses the history of The Forth from various earlier sources.

'It was in use by the 1500s, being used for the playing of bowls and archery. It began as a square field of over four acres, fenced to keep animals out, and used by people of all ages for their leisure: a playground for children, dancing square, 'trysting ground' for lovers, meeting place for the guilds before they built their own guild halls, and a place for the old to stroll and enjoy the view'.

After 1660, the Forth House was extended, becoming a large tavern.

We learn that the citizens used to enjoy the ancient game of bowls in summertime. Political meetings in later days were sometimes held in the enclosure. *Oliver's Plan of Newcastle*, published in 1830 shows that the 'Forth joined the Cattle Market, and was situated between the (Gunner lower, which was removed in 1885, and the Infirmary, which still stands in the place it occupied in 1830. Neville Street, the Central Station, and the North-Eastern Railway, in fact, have taken the place of the once popular resort'. Three sketches of the old Forth Tavern, taken from original drawings preserved in a book that belonged to the late John Waller, proprietor of the Turf Hotel, Newcastle, were made in 1843, shortly before the place was pulled down and the entire locality transformed. See below. 'It was in this tavern and under the veranda in front of it, that the citizens were accustomed to gather of an evening, there to watch the sports which were proceeding on the green sward of the Forth itself'.

Mr. Richardson's History of the Forth reveals how the inn was the place to go for the best night out:

The Forth has probably been in use as a place of recreation from a very early period…our mayors and aldermen of the earlier days of Queen Elizabeth do not appear to have thought it beneath their dignity to witness and reward the exertions of "the fellyshpe of a shyp [of] Albroughe, dansyng in the Fyrthe," or even the pranks of a "player," who, it is gravely stated, was rewarded "for playing with a hobie-horse in the Firthe, before the maior and his brethren"; and, though it is not specially mentioned where the ceremony took place, yet we can hardly doubt that the bearward of Lord Monteagle, "him that had the lyon," and the "tumbler that tumbled before Mr. Maior and his brethren," one and all exhibited the capacities of themselves or of their respective charges in the presence of these worshipful sightseers in this ancient place of recreation… Archery, too. it would seem, has been practised here by the stalwart youths of the town, for in July, 1567, we have a charge "for making up the buttes in the Fyrthe." It seems probable, in fact, that the Forth has also been the campus martius of the town, or, at least, one of the places appropriated to the purposes of military array…

About 1657, a bowling-green and house for the keeper, was made by contribution in part of the Forth; around which on 29th July, 1680, the Corporation ordered a wall to be built, and lime trees brought out of Holland to be planted therein. On 25th Sept., 1682, there was an order of the same body "to make the Forth House suitable for entertainment, with a cellar convenient, and a handsome room, & c."

We go on to learn how the records of the guilds reveal 'many amusing entries whereby we observe that they did not neglect creature comforts, or spurn the aid of the drinking glass or of the fragrant weed'. As might be expected, the proximity of a tavern and a bowling-green 'tempted many from their sterner duties; so we find that while one slips away to enjoy a pipe, a second is detected "playing at bowels" in the green'.

For more details, see https://1stnorth.co.uk/the-forth-newcastle

The original forth.

***The Forth Hotel**, 14 St Mary's Pl, Newcastle upon Tyne NE1 7PG*
Telephone: 0191 211 1140

The Free Trade Inn,
Ouseburn

The Free Trade is a pub that has changed very little over the years, and why would it? With its shabby charm and longstanding dedication to real ale and cider, as well as offering the best view of the Newcastle-Gateshead quayside from a beer garden…[https://www.ouseburn.co.uk/directory/the-free-trade/]

The former beerhouse probably opened shortly after the introduction of the 1830 Beer Act. Bought by Henry Davidson of the White Lion Brewery in 1888. Rebuilt in 1896 to designs by Oswald & Son. Their original design had two large decorative gables in Queen Anne revival style with ball finials and hooded canopy over the door. Inside the bar had a V-shaped counter to echo the shape of the building. There was a club room upstairs. Henry Davidson opted for a cheaper design which increased the size of the tenant's accommodation and replaced the proposed club room with bedrooms. The façade hardly had any decoration apart from facings round the windows and a parapet inscribed with the name Free Trade. In 1899 Matthew Wood, brewer from South Shields bought it. In 1911 there were structural alterations. The tenant's kitchen became a parlour, the bar counter was extended and the family room became part of the main bar. In 1919 the Free Trade became a Newcastle Breweries pub. In 1937 more internal partitions were removed. It almost closed in 1947 when Newcastle Breweries applied to transfer the licence to a new pub to be built in Sackville Road. The Free Trade was not granted a full publican's licence until 1963. It is still a free house. Little of the original interior survives apart from the basic form of the bar counter and part of the back bar fitting'.

[Source: https://sitelines.newcastle.gov.uk/SMR/15838]

Free art at the Free Trade – gregjonesart.com

St Lawrence Road, *Byker, Newcastle upon Tyne, NE6 1AP • Telephone: 0191 265 5764*

The Hancock

Formerly known as Bierrex, the pub is located by the north side of the Civic Centre. It is named after Newcastle-born John Hancock (1808-1890), who was a founder of the brilliant Great North Museum: Hancock, nearby.

John Hancock was a British naturalist, ornithologist, taxidermist and landscape architect. Working during the golden age of taxidermy when mounted animals became a popular part of Victorian era interior design, Hancock is considered the father of modern taxidermy.

A taxidermy tableau titled The Struggle with the Quarry by John Hancock 1808–1890), at the Great North (Hancock) Museum, Newcastle. The tableau was created during or before 1851, and was shown at the 1851 Great Exhibition. The tableau shows a gyrfalcon (Falco rusticolus) attacking a heron (Ardea cinerea).

This exhibit is on permanent display at a public museum in the United Kingdome. Thus it comes under Panoramafreiheit. See Freedom of panorama, and section 62 of Copyright, Designs and Patents Act 1988.

The Hancock, *2A Hancock Street, Newcastle-upon-Tyne NE2 4PU*
Telephone: 0191 281 5653

The Hotspur

Situated opposite Haymarket bus station and Eldon Square, with the universities close by; Newcastle University Folk Club (members past and present) play on Tuesday nights. The interior has recently been refurbished and is much enhanced without losing character. Dating back to 1892, the Hotspur pub opened the same year Newcastle United was founded.

In the past, university staff congregated in the Hotspur as part of strike action over pension plans, pay cuts and revised contracts at their universities. During the strikes, the Hotspur became an alternative lecture theatre, where 'teach out' sessions took place.

The Hotspur, 103 Percy Street, Newcastle upon Tyne NE1 7RY
Telephone: (0191) 232 4352

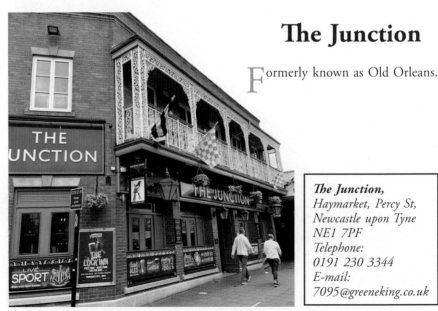

The Junction

Formerly known as Old Orleans.

The Junction,
Haymarket, Percy St,
Newcastle upon Tyne
NE1 7PF
Telephone:
0191 230 3344
E-mail:
7095@greeneking.co.uk

Lady Greys

Formerly the Adelphi. Located on Shakespeare Street, next door to the Theatre Royal. The interior is a retro style with dark wood and vintage photos throughout.

Some inspired marketing here!

Lady Greys, *20 Shakespeare Street, Newcastle Upon Tyne, NE1 6AQ*
Telephone: 0191 232 5932
E-mail: info@ladygreys.co.uk
Website: www.ladygreys.co.uk

The Mile Castle

Formerly Sports Café; Lloyd's No. 1 Bar. Previously this was also the head office of the TSB Bank.

The current name of this JD Wetherspoon pub obviously references the mile castles which studded the length of nearby Hadrian's Wall. Under Hadrian (r. 117 to 138) and Antoninus Pius (r. 138 to 161), two walls were built to deter and keep out the belligerent Caledonians. A line stretching across modern Northumberland from Newcastle-upon-Tyne (Pons Aelius) to Carlisle on the Solway was the new limit of empire; a line which, constructed in the 120s and 130s AD, was to become Hadrian's Wall. The monumental wall extended 73 miles comprising ditch, a thicket of spikes, a stone wall, a sequence of forts, mile castles and observation turrets, and a permanent garrison of up to 8,000 men.

The bridge and its fort at Newcastle were built at the north end of Cade's Road, which ran from Brough to York and the fort of Concangis (Chester-le-Street). The bridge was the only one outside Rome named after an emperor (Hadrian). Strategically it commanded an excellent position at the northern bridgehead of the Tyne.

In 2010, to commemorate the 1600th anniversary of the end of Roman rule in Britain, a series of 500 beacons were lit along the length of the wall. 13 March 2010. From geograph.org.uk. Photographer Gary Dickson

A stone dedicated to empress Julia Domna dated 213 has been excavated nearby. A dedication to emperor Hadrian's mother, Domitia Paulina, attests the presence of the Cohors Ulpia Traiana Cugernorum civium Romanorum (The Cohort of Ulpian Cugerni, Trajan's Own) as being stationed at Pons Aelius at the beginning of the third century. *The Notitia Dignitatum* records the Cohors I Cornoviorum (The First Cohort of Cornovii) as being present at the fort in the beginning of the fifth century. These were raised from among the Cornovii tribe from Cheshire and Shropshire, and were the only native British unit known to have been stationed on Hadrian's Wall. A stone tablet was found in Hanover Square that records that the Cohors I Thracum worked on the *vallum*.

Only two piers of Pons Aelii have been found but altars to Neptune and Oceanus were dredged from the river. The Bridge was 735 feet long and 16 feet wide, the piers had cutwaters up and downstream and there appears to have been ten piers and two abutments. The Swing Bridge, constructed 1868-76, now occupies the site. The Newcastle Arts Centre occupies the site of a Roman mile castle.

The Mile Castle is one of Newcastle's biggest venues. It extends over three floors, each with seating areas and their own bar.

https://www. jdwetherspoon. com/pubs/all-pubs/ england/tyne-and-wear/the-mile-castle-newcastle-upon-tyne

Information inside the Mile Castle to reflect on. This is typical of Wetherspoon pubs where there is always an effort to inform on the history of their houses.

The Mile Castle, *19-25 Westgate Road &, Grainger St, Newcastle upon Tyne NE1 5XU • Telephone: 0191 211 1160 • E-mail: p6180@jdwetherspoon.co.uk*

The Newcastle Arms

A single room pub next door to St James' Park and Chinatown known locally as the "Top Arms"; obviously it is very busy on match days and beer festival opening nights.

The Newcastle Arms, 55-57 St Andrews Street, Newcastle upon Tyne NE1 5SE
Telephone: 0191 260 2421 • E-mail: alistair-platt@hotmail.com
Website: www.pubsnewcastle.co.uk/NewcastleArms.htm

The Old George

Claims to be the oldest pub in Newcastle dating back to 1582, with its low beamed ceilings and capacious open fireplaces.

Inside the Old George

The Old George is Newcastle's last remaining coaching inn. Apparently, this was Charles I's local while he was being held prisoner by the Scottish Covenanters, staying at Oliver Cromwell's pleasure in an open prison in nearby Shield Field for ten months in 1646-1647; there's even a replica here of the chair in which Charles used to sit before he got headless. Not only was the doomed king allowed a pint but he was also permitted to play 'goff' (golf) in the Shield Field area. Some say he was imprisoned in from May 1646 to February 1647 in Anderson Place in a building which no longer exists today.

Many visitors have claimed to see a ghostly figure sitting in the chair. Footsteps have been heard in the bar when it is closed. A man with a dog has been seen standing at the bar [and most hilarious of all] in the main function room staff have reported feeling nauseous. (Rob Kirkup, 2009, *Ghostly Tyne & Wear*, pages 87-88).

In 1644, during the English Civil War, the Scots invaded England and attacked Newcastle. The city was besieged for three months until its defences were finally breached. To thank the city for their brave, yet unsuccessful, efforts, Charles gave Newcastle the motto 'Fortiter Defendit Triumphans' to be added to its coat of arms.

Old George Inn, *Cloth Market, Newcastle upon Tyne, Tyne & Wear, NE1 1EZ*
Telephone: 0191 260 3035 • E-mail: oldgeorge.newcastle@stonegatepubs.com
Website: www.oldgeorgeinnnewcastle.co.uk

The Percy Arms

Bought and altered by Vaux in 1939. Sadly, the exterior tiles have gone but the 100-year-old weather vane survives. The name of the pub and the street derives from the House of Percy, an English noble family who were one of the most powerful noble families in northern England for much of the Middle Ages, known for their long rivalry with the House of Neville.

The Percy Arms, Percy St, Newcastle upon Tyne NE1 7RW
Telephone: 0191 222 1412 • E-mail: percyarms.newcastle@stonegategroup.co.uk
Website: www.percyarmsnewcastle.co.uk

'Pleased to Meet You…'

The name is inspired by the chorus of the Rolling Stones' *Sympathy for the Devil:* 'Pleased to meet you; Hope you guess my name; But what's puzzling you is the nature of my game'.

Keith Richards – a Ron Wood print, signed, named and numbered limited edition to 295.

Pleased to Meet You, *C41-45 High Bridge, NE1 1EW*

87

Pumphrey's Blues Café

Opened in 2020 right next to the Old George.

'Introducing the all-new Blues Cafe Newcastle, a sleek update of rough and ready Mississippi blues bar, spread across two floors of a Grade II Listed Building bringing a touch of Southern Soul to Newcastle city centre!' Apparently the cheapest beer in town; Motown music too.

Pumphrey's Blues Café , *44 Cloth Market, Newcastle Upon Tyne, United Kingdom, NE1 1EE*

The Quayside

A JD Wetherspoon pub. This is what the Newcastle-Gateshead website says about Quayside, the place with its numerous bars, pubs and restaurants:

Flanking both sides of the River Tyne, Quayside is a fantastic place for scenic strolls and bike rides, a spot of sightseeing or a meal at one of the top restaurants on Newcastle-Gateshead Quayside. As night time approaches, choose from vibrant Quayside bars where you can sup beer, sip cocktails and admire great views.

In the past, the Quayside played a central part of Newcastle's industrial history and heritage, serving as a commercial dockside. Coal was also ferried down to the Quayside via the Victoria Tunnels, which are now a popular tourist attraction, while factories such as the Baltic Flour Mill and Hoults Yard pottery, which have both since been transformed, flourished nearby at Gateshead Quays and Ouseburn. After much of the industry moved on, the area underwent a huge regeneration in the early 2000s, and has since become a hub of arts and culture for the North East, as well as a home to many of the region's best bars and pubs.

One of the many Quayside bars and pubs, the Pitcher & Piano

The Quayside, *35–37 The Close, Quayside, Newcastle upon Tyne NE1 3RN*
Telephone: 01912111050 • E-mail: p1810@jdwetherspoon.co.uk
Website: www.jdwetherspoon.com/pubs/

The Redhouse

On Newcastle's Quayside, this Grade II listed building gives a brilliant view of the Tyne Bridge. A sign on the building gives its date as the fifteenth century. Also known as Redhouse Pie, Mash & Ale House, formerly Bob Trollops, Redhouse; the Beehive.

What's the connection between Blackbeard the Caribbean pirate and the Red House?

Known as the "Newcastle Pirate", Edward Robinson sailed with Blackbeard during the good old days of piracy in the early 1700s. Local author Paul Brown has uncovered the true facts about Edward Robinson in his book *Sins Dyed In Blood: In Search of the Newcastle Pirate*. Robinson was reputedly born in a pub called the Beehive, now the Redhouse, on Newcastle's Quayside, and fled to sea to become a pirate after slitting a man's throat and dumping the body in the Tyne. But there's more: Paul's research took him to Charleston, South Carolina, where Robinson was tried for piracy after his involvement in a series of pirate raids as one of Blackbeard's crew.

Inside the Red House

However, he carelessly fell out with his captain, and was marooned and left for dead on a tiny desert island. Robinson was eventually rescued by another notorious pirate captain, Stede Bonnet, and resumed his piratical ways until, in 1718, he was captured off the coast of America and sentenced to death for his crimes.

"You caused your terror to be on all that haunt the sea," the Judge told him, "and your sins are dyed in blood." In November 1718, Robinson, Stede Bonnet and 28 other pirates were hanged at White Point in Charleston. "There's a stone monument marking the spot where they were hanged, and where Edward Robinson's story came to an end, 4,000 miles from home", concludes Brown.

April Wright-Atkinson says on Flickr:

At the time it was my mum and dad's restaurant. I was a year old. They had opened The Redhouse a year earlier and it was the first place you could get dinner after 9pm! It was very popular with businessmen and footballers. We still have some of the original cutlery and crockery with the Redhouse logo on them and also the menus and wine lists.

Sandhill has been used as a quayside since Roman times and was named such because it used to be a veritable hill of sand when the tide was out. The land was gradually reclaimed by dumping of rubbish there from 12th century to 15th century.

The Redhouse,
32 Sandhill, Newcastle
Upon Tyne, NE1 3JF
Telephone: 0191 261 1037
E-mail:
info@theredhousencl.co.uk

The Ship,
Ouseburn

A nod towards the historic importance of river craft in the commercial development and heritage of the Ouseburn Valley.

Graffiti opposite the Ship

Graffiti on the side of the Ship

The Ship, *Stepney Bank, Newcastle upon Tyne NE1 2PW • Telephone: 0191 222 0878*

The Split Chimp Micropub

Established in May 2015 by Mark Hall as the first and original Micropub in Newcastle. It is ingeniously shoe-horned into a refurbished railway arch behind Newcastle Central Station opposite the site of the former Federation Brewery. Upstairs there is a 31ft-long skittle lane: a first for a micropub, which occasionally hosts occasional live music?

In Feb 2019 Mark opened a second Micropub in the refurbished Spanish City in Whitley Bay called The Split Chimp Ale House, and in May 2021 opened a third in Seaton Delaval, The Split Chimp Tavern. 'Three pubs, in three counties, within cycling distance of each other'.

What's a split chimp? Nothing sinister: it's a small wedge of wood placed at the back of a cask to allow it to be tilted.

Inside the Split Chimp

Split Chimp, *Arch 7, Westgate Road, Newcastle upon Tyne NE1 1SA*
E-mail: mark@splitchimp.pub
Website: www.splitchimp.pub

The Strawberry

Famous for being full of Newcastle United memorabilia. 'We are one of the oldest and much-loved pubs in Newcastle. We also serve a canny pint'. Check out the toilet seat in the ladies too.

https://foursquare.com/v/the-strawberry/4b6dd2eaf964a5204a932ce3

Ever since 1892 supporters have flocked to St James' Park and the Strawberry; the term 'football fan' hadn't yet been coined 128 years ago - they were called 'enthusiasts' then. 'I recommend you a visit here, even if you're not a Magpies fan/follower if only for the great staff and the well documented toilet seat (Trip Advisor post)'.

There has been a building here since around 1840 – and a pub since 1859, originally intended to cater for people wandering around the surrounding pleasure gardens. The pub's name and the street name, Strawberry Place, is thought to derive from the nuns of nearby St Bartholomew's who grew strawberries on plantations in the area and made strawberry wine.

A busy match day

The Newcastle Chronicle tells us that St James' Hall, a 4,000-capacity boxing hall, was just over the road from the football ground. Opened in 1930, it hosted up to six fights a week. World heavyweight champion Sonny Liston sparred there in 1963, and all-in wrestling was popular here for a while. St James' Park was developed at the most southern end of Castle Leazes. Historically, a hospital and chapel named St. James' stood near to where the Hancock Museum building now stands. In 1542, the master of St. Mary's and St. James granted a lease of land and plots that extended to Castle Leazes. St. James Place was later built on the site. The original football ground was built by 1880 on what was grazing land, bordered by Leazes Terrace, and near Town Moor, and used by Newcastle Rangers. In 1892 Newcastle East End took on the lease of St James' Park and became Newcastle United that year.

The first match on the site, a practice match, had kicked off in 1880 with Newcastle Rangers, who moved north of the River Tyne after forming in 1878 and initially playing on the Drill Field in Gateshead. Newcastle Rangers moved again to Byker in 1882, returning in 1884 before folding. West End Football Club stepped in, taking up the tenancy two years later in 1886. In April 1895 Newcastle United hosted a women's exhibition match at St James' Park with 8,000 people coming to watch.

The city's big clubs, Newcastle East End and West End FC, merged and formally took up residence at St. James' Park in 1892 - finally becoming Newcastle United.

The Gallowgate End has a grim history, as its name might suggest. The "Gallows Hole" was here: in 1650, 22 people – including 15 "witches" – were hanged in one day. In 1783, William Alexander was hanged for forging a bank note and, in 1786, Henry Jennings was executed for stealing horses. The last hanging took place in 1844: Mark Sherwood of Blandford Street murdered his wife and was taken by cart to the gallows, in front of the posh Leazes Terrace - sitting on his own coffin.

That toilet

The Strawberry, 7-8 Strawberry Pl, Newcastle upon Tyne NE1 4SF
Telephone: 0191 232 6865

Swarley's

S warley's is the latest, non-controversial name of this famous pub, formerly the Black Boy and then the Blackie Boy, both inspired by the local blacksmiths but nevertheless are names which clearly have the power to offend; Coffy

When it was the Blackie Boy

Johney was another former name. Renamed in 2021 Swarley's is after Richard Swarley, one of the former proprietors who ran a debating club on the premises in the 18th century, which counted engraver Thomas Bewick among its members.

Women were strictly *verboten* in Swarleys Club. However, according to www. friendsaction.co.uk

'Rough lower class women, along with other ruffians, tramps and degenerates of the town centre were apparently allowed in one room only, known as Hells Kitchen, in the nearby establishment named The Flying Horse. Euphy Scott, Queen of the fishwives and Owld Judy, guardian of the town hutch, along with blind Willie Purvis also drank here. Landlord Ralf ruled his clients with an iron fist. Any arguments erupting meant doors would be locked until calm was restored. Serious breachers of Hells Kitchen etiquette were punished by a six months ban'.

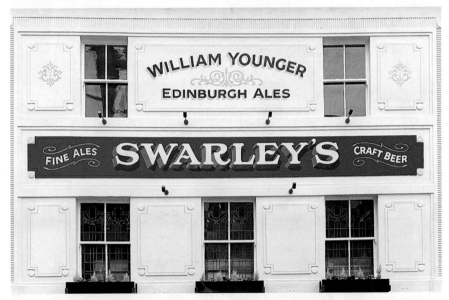

Award winning signage. New signs for a renamed pub have been recognised with a Lord Mayor's Award in Newcastle. The sign painting, by Ash Willerton and Alex Richardson, took top prize in the "Frontage Transformation" category. The work was carried out within a larger initiative to transform the historic Bigg Market area in Newcastle-upon-Tyne.

Owners Ollie and Harry Vaulkhard resorted to the history books for their new name and are keen to point out that "We are not deleting Blackie Boy from the history books and reference will be made to its history inside the venue and in its window displays. We want to create a beautiful, traditional pub in the heart of Newcastle, one steeped in history that will contribute to the continued success of the Bigg Market." The Vaulkhard Group have restored the façade to accentuate its art-deco features and renovating the interior to recreate a traditional Victoriana-style pub.

Coffee Johnny aka Coffy Johnny and John Oliver (1829 – 1900) enjoys eternal fame due to his appearance in the 6th verse George Ridley's *'The Blaydon Races'*. Coffee Johnny was a blacksmith in the village of Winlaton, a trumpeter in the Winlaton Brass Band, a bare-knuckle boxer and all-round Geordie celebrity. He was known for his tall height and for wearing a white top hat which can be seen in photographs and in William Irving's painting 'Blaydon Races'.

Local history archives contain anecdotal evidence that he was nicknamed Coffy because he always used to have a cup of coffee before going to school. There is also anecdotal evidence that he may have been of mixed race, hence his "coffee" coloured skin. Furthermore, it has been suggested that it was derived from his birth mother, Sara Koeffer's, surname. Sara was a German lady residing at Ravensworth Castle, near to Winlaton.

A groat or tuppence is the name of a long-defunct English coin. This coin had been in circulation since being minted at the time of Edward I (r. 1272-1307).

A silver groat from the reign of Edward I (1272–1307)

Swarley's, *11 Groat Market, Newcastle Upon Tyne, NE1 1UQ*
Website: www.blackieboy.co.uk

Three Bulls Heads

Located in Eldon Garden Shopping Centre. The Percy Street Brewery was behind the Three Bulls' Heads which was run by Henry Rudolphus Ritzema from 1850 to 1853. The brewery was then taken over by George Southern for a short time; it had a two-horse-power steam engine and could produce 35 half barrels per brewing. In 1984 Bass owned the Three Bulls' Heads. What you see today is a complete rebuild. It's very handy for St James' Park: the pub is out to capture all the match-day atmosphere.

https://sitelines.newcastle.gov.uk/SMR/6539 gives us the following information:

Bourne records that there was a Chapel of the Garrison (or "Chapel House") in Castle Garth. By 1736 this was the site of the Three Bulls Heads Inn. When the Black Gate was occupied by John Pickles (he occupied the Black Gate until 1661), vintner, he also ran a tavern there which may have been the precursor of the later Two Bulls Heads. Between 1787 and 1789 two public houses are associated with the Black Gate, the Blue Bell and an unnamed establishment run by John Fife, bear-brewer. In 1790 the latter passed to another John Fife, staymaker, and was known as the Three Bulls Heads, Blackgate. It disappears from the directories five years later, only to re-emerge the following century as the Two Bulls Heads. By the mid-18th century much of the basement of the Keep was in use as beer cellars for the inn… The Three Bulls Heads served as a focal point for the community around it. Tradesmen in the Garth were "initiated" at a general meeting of their fellow traders at the inn. A beer cellar was dug for the tavern in 1752. In 1855 the Three Bulls Heads went to auction. It contained cellars, a bar, newsroom, tap rooms, parlour and quoits area with a 12 half-barrel brewery attached. The pub closed in 1892. Nolan suggested that a cellar built for this inn in 1752 was located during archaeological excavations in railway arch 27, occupying the space between the sites of two Anglo Saxon chapels or churches.

The Three Bulls Head in the milk market

Three Bulls Heads, *57 Percy Street, Newcastle Upon Tyne NE1 7RN*
Telephone: 01912602984 • E-mail: threebullsheads.newcastle@stonegategroup.co.uk

The Town Mouse

The Town Mouse micro pub, a former coffee shop, can be found in the basement of a 200-year-old building on St. Mary's Place down the stairs next to the 5 Swans Pub; a few minutes' walk from both Haymarket and Newcastle City Hall. One of its laudable aims is to help champion North East microbrewers and their unique beers; another is to pay living wages. The interior is inspired by the traditional ale houses of Belgium and basement pubs from Ireland and Berlin.

The Town Mouse, Basement, 11 St Mary's Place, Newcastle, NE1 7PG
E-mail: info@townmousealehouse
Website: www. townmousealehouse.co.uk

The Town Wall

The Town Wall occupies a Grade II listed building which was once home and studio of famous Northumberland artist, naturalist and engraver Thomas Bewick (1753 – 1828). It gets its name from the fact that the site once formed part of Newcastle's original fortified boundaries. Former names are Bewick House and Coco V. All the signage is hand painted on the walls – 'a lovely touch'.

The pub is mentioned in records dating back as early as 1280; the building's boundaries include the site of the original Gunner Tower which was built by the ancient family of Swinburn. In 1821 the building was converted into a hall for the incorporated company of Slaters and Tylers; the workmen found a large haul of shillings and sixpences of Edward I.

Bewick was born in the village of Mickley, Northumberland, near Newcastle upon Tyne. He turned his hand to all kinds of work such as engraving cutlery,

making the wood blocks for advertisements, and illustrating children's books. He gradually moved towards illustrating, writing and publishing his own books, not least the beautifully illustrated *A General History of Quadrupeds* (1790). Bewick is best known for his *A History of British Birds* (two volumes: *History and Description of Land Birds* in 1797 and *History and Description of Water Birds* in 1804), the forerunner of all modern field guides. He also illustrated fine editions of *Aesop's Fables* throughout his life.

THOMAS BEWICK BIRTHPLACE MUSEUM IN CHERRYBURN NORTHUMBERLAND. The kitchen is currently occupied by an art and audio installation called Conference for the Birds featuring seven giant birds (cuckoo, great black-backed gull, roseate tern, tree sparrow, blackbird, heron and dotterel) as depicted by Thomas in his wood engravings.

The Newcastle town wall was built during the 13th and 14th centuries, and was approximately 2 mi long, at least 6.5 ft thick, up to 25 ft high, and had six main gates: Close Gate, West Gate, New Gate, Pilgrim Gate, Pandon Gate and Sand Gate. It also had seventeen towers, as well as several smaller turrets and postern gates. The town wall was kept in good repair whilst there was a threat of invasion from Scottish armies but with the decline of the border wars between England and Scotland, the wall was allowed to become dilapidated.

The Town Wall, *Pink Lane, Newcastle upon Tyne NE1 5HX*
Telephone: 0191 232 3000 • E-mail: info@thetownwall.com

The Tyne Bar

The Tyne Bar and the Bridge

The Tyne has, by common consent, been one of Newcastle's most liked independent pubs since it first opened in November 1994 and is still as popular today. It is located just under the Glasshouse Bridge at the confluence of the Rivers Ouse and Tyne. According to www.thetyne.com 'In its former life, The Tyne Bar was known as The Ship Tavern; a notorious establishment better known for the horizontal refreshment on offer in the rooms upstairs than for the [vertical] liquid refreshment at the bar'. The building dates from 1895 to replace the original Ship Tavern, which opened here in 1850, but was destroyed by a fire. The pub was known locally as the 'Bottom Ship', to differentiate it from the other Ship Inn, which is located nearby, higher up the Ouseburn on Stepney Bank.

The Tyne Bar window when it was the Ship

In 1994 the pub was renovated and renamed 'The Tyne'; it is run by the same people who managed the Barley Mow and the Egypt Cottage.

The Tyne Bar is on Newcastle's Local List of Buildings of Local Architectural or Historic Interest.

The earliest reference in a trade directory is in 1824 when William Smith was the "innkeeper of the Ship at Glasshouse". The very first directory of Newcastle by John Robert Boyle in 1778 records Richard Benson, innkeeper at the Ship, "Ewesburn" but we don't know

Inside the Tyne Bar

The Egypt Cottage signage

if this is the "bottom Ship" or the "top Ship". The early directories record the pub's name as the Ship and it isn't until about 1857 that we find it referred to as the Ship Tavern.

The Ship has changed breweries several times and its owners have included Naters Sandyford Brewery, Arrol's, Vaux, Maclay & Co, Hammonds and Bass Charrington before it became a free house in 1978 and was renamed the Tyne in 1994.

'Trade directories show us that the innkeeper at the Ship Tavern from about 1900 to 1920 was Percival Bagnall. The 1901 census (not unusually for the times) reveals that innkeeper wasn't Bagnall's only occupation as he and his two eldest sons are described as wherrymen. Wherries were clinker-built, general purpose river vessels for carrying raw materials and finished goods as well as acting as lighters to carry goods to and from visiting ships. Originally they were simply powered by the tide and punting poles or oars and sometimes by simple sailing rigs. Strings of wherries would be towed by tugs and by the late nineteenth century could be powered by engines. Typically, wherries would be about fifty feet long, weighing 35 to 40 tons, although they did vary in size. By the twentieth century there were over 200 companies and individuals operating on the River Tyne. The last remaining wherry, Elswick No.2, was withdrawn from service in the early 1970s and is now at Beamish Museum.

Working on the river could be hazardous: during the 1840s and 50s, on average, one body a week was recovered from both the Newcastle and Gateshead quaysides. On the Newcastle side, the bodies would be taken to the Dead House which stood near the mouth of the Ouseburn. Next door to the Dead House was the River Police Station and nearby was the Stone Cellars, an old public house where many of the inquests were held on the bodies removed from the river'.

- The Ship Tavern and the Mouth of the Ouseburn

The two striking windows

*Image by kind permission of the artist, Yvette Earl; for lots more
of her work see www.yvette-earl.com*

The Tyne Bar, *Maling Street, Newcastle upon Tyne, Newcastle upon Tyne, NE6 1LP*
Telephone: 0191 265 2550

Urban Garden,
Quayside

One of Newcastle's Brewdogs, outside but weatherproof.

Quayside Seaside, *Quayside, Newcastle upon Tyne NE1 3DH, UK*

The Victoria Comet

Over the road from the station, the Victoria Comet has been the Victoria and Comet in the '60s (Duddingtons Ales); a Yates Wine Lodge in 1974 and it went Irish in the 1990s with Durty Nellie's (1994) and O'Neil's (1996). In 2014 it was nicely converted to Nicholson's most northerly pub in England.

It's alleged association with the 1972 film *Dirty Harry* and Michael Caine is celebrated inside with photographs of various shoots. (There is some confusion with the Half Moon in Bigg Market which is actually named in the film). Having travelled by train from London, hitman Jack Carter crosses over the road and walks straight into the crowded pub where he famously asks for a drink served in "a thin glass".

The Half Moon in Bigg Market – mural outside Pumphreys. See also p. 152.

Shooting a Michael Caine scene in 'Get Carter'

> **The Victoria Comet,** *38 Neville Street, Newcastle-Upon-Tyne, Tyne And Wear, NE1 5DF*
> *Telephone: 0191 261 7921*

The building that houses The Victoria Comet has been used as a pub since the 1800s — indeed, it once housed two pubs, The Victoria on the left, and The Comet on the right. In 1929 the two were merged by Deuchars, and became The Victoria and Comet Hotel.

The Waiting Rooms

Formerly Long Bar. Close to Central Station, hence the name.

The Waiting Room, 39-47 Westgate Road, Newcastle upon Tyne, NE1 5SG
Telephone: 0191 2615771
E-mail: waitingrooms.900751@bermondseypubco.com
Website: https://www.craft-pubs.co.uk/the-waiting-rooms-newcastle

WC,
Bigg Market

'there's nothing bog-standard about it' – Newcastle Chronicle

The *Chronicle* reports that 'The city centre's iconic Victorian underground lavatories have been transformed into a high-end wine bar called W.C'. marking a high point in the street's regeneration. The 1898 building closed in 2012. It continues 'that trademark elevated glass roof is back - all new - and floods the bar with light'. Owner Steve Blair insists that 'those initials - besides standing for Water Closet - also represent Wine and Charcuterie as well as Wine and Cocktails, which sum up his business'.

Outside

Inside

Before

After

Underground public toilets were introduced in the United Kingdom during the reign of Queen Victoria, in built-up urban areas where no space was available to provide them above ground. The facilities were accessible by steps, and lit by glass bricks on the pavement above. Local health boards often built underground public toilets to a high standard, although provisions were, unsurprisingly, higher for men than women. Most have been closed as they do not have disabled access, and were more prone to vandalism and 'sexual encounters', especially when there is no attendant. A few remain in London, but others have been converted into alternative uses such as cafes, bars, as in Newcastle, and even dwellings.

WC Newcastle, *Bigg Market,*
Newcastle-upon-Tyne NE1 1UW

The WC Gin Closet

A gin bar located in the old (as in former, not age) ladies' toilets in a fine Georgian property on High Bridge in the Bigg Market area of Newcastle, reputed to be the smallest gin bar in the UK measuring 11 square metres. It comes courtesy of the owners of The WC (see above) also in the Bigg Market, and is described as a 'small, dark and opulent 'with a speakeasy vibe.

It can seat up to 15 guests, with buttons on the wall for customers to order their gins direct from their seats.

Yes, it does actually have its own toilet.

Before   *After and now*

The WC Gin Closet, *41 High Bridge, Newcastle upon Tyne, NE1 1EG*
Telephone: 0191 5808 508 • E-mail: info@wcnewcastle.co.uk

THE PUBS OF GATESHEAD

During the nineteenth century, Durham and Northumberland were top of the pops in the league of drunkenness. Temperance Halls were established to valiantly try to alleviate this and its attendant anti-social behaviour and domestic violence. In 1846 there were a mere 73 adult teetotallers in Gateshead along with 49 juveniles, and only four ministers.

Drunkenness increased in line with the population. In 1851 one in every 168 people of Gateshead was convicted of drunkenness. Immigrants, especially the Irish and Scots, may have contributed to the drunkenness but it's probably just another manifestation of the Englishman's habit of blaming everything bad on foreigners rather than himself - a character flaw which persists today: ask any Irishman, Jew or gypsy. According to George Lucas, a temperance supporter, there were 170 public houses in the 1860s. The population of Gateshead was only 35,000 at this time; that's 170 pubs for 35,000 people (205 people per pub) and now in the extended borough of Gateshead, comprising some 200,000 people there are fewer than 200 pubs (1,000 people per pub).

As John Boothroyd says in his excellent *The Old Pubs of Gateshead* (2014), Gateshead is a bit unusual as British towns go: 'few pubs are of any great age, few pubs could be described as grand and most of those standing in 1945 have since been demolished'. A little harsh and dystopian perhaps; despite forever living 'in Newcastle's shadow', Gateshead does have its own high points in pubs and civic amenities, not least the wonderful Sage: 'Sage Gateshead is an international music centre and renowned conference and event venue... It is for artists, for audiences and for the North'.

In the past, football was important in the pubs of Gateshead: New Gateshead Football Club came out of the New Gateshead Inn; while Albert Blue Star FC has its origins in the Albert.

Nineteenth century population explosion and the labour demands of the Industrial Revolution caused the population to grow every decade from 1820 until 1920 from a tiny 12,000 to a huge 125,000. With working men and their families came pubs. Boothroyd concludes 'Gateshead's old pubs are a reflection of a town built around industry and commuting where the showpiece centre lay elsewhere... the Gateshead of the old pubs was not pretty'. Well, let's have a look...

The Barley Mow,
Vigo Lane, Gateshead

Sitelines, (www.twsitelines.info), describes this best.

*T*his site has long been the location of a public house, but when it was established it was part of a tiny settlement to the south of Birtley called Brown's Buildings. The old pub had been called the Fox & Hounds, but changed its name to the Barley Mow during the 19th century. The dense settlement around the pub now did not appear until around the time the pub was rebuilt, and so in all probability the settlement took its name from the institution – making it of historical as well as architectural importance to the area. This new development must have stimulated the rebuilding, in order to give more space and better accommodation for the potential new clientele. It is a distinguished and stately building in red-brown brick, with a special and distinctive hipped roof of green clay roman tiles to complement, graced with a single, simple tall chimney... The most outstanding element of the design, however, is the corner turret, with curved bay windows stretching around at least a full semi-circle. It is a wonderful way to finish a corner, and makes a significant contribution to the impact of the establishment in the street scene as a navigable landmark, as well as helping to create an attractive building. In 1925 Mark West was the landlord, however, this would have been before the pub was rebuilt.

Image by kind permission of the artist, Yvette Earl;
for lots more of her work see www.yvette-earl.com

The Central Bar,
Gateshead

A historic pub interior of national importance - CAMRA

On Half Moon Lane and Hills Street corner in Gateshead, it was built in 1856, and became a hotel around 1890. The Central is Grade II listed and is nicknamed "The Coffin", because of its unusual shape. Let CAMRA do the talking:

This imposing corner-site building between the Tyne and High Level bridges dates from 1854, designed by architect M. Thompson as premises for a wine merchant, Alderman Potts. It became a hotel about 1890 and this is, no doubt, the date when the star feature, the Buffet Bar, was fitted out. This is now styled the Whisky Bar thanks to the wide range of said spirit on offer. It has a U-shaped counter with an impressive front of broad segmental arches and a tremendously ornate bar-back. There is also fixed seating, half-height panelling, etched glass in the doors, a fine ceiling and deep plasterwork frieze. This room is open Fri–Sat evenings but may be viewed at other times on request. Elsewhere, panelling survives in the hallway staircase whilst the public bar has further panelling and a partially old bar counter. The sharp angle of the site explains the unusual triangular shape of the snug which is set beyond the Buffet Bar. It has impressively large etched windows, giving it a light and airy feel. After a long period of neglect the Central was carefully restored in 2010 and is now a haven for real ale and cider.

(Taken from https://pubheritage.camra.org.uk/pubs/158)

You can see footage of Gateshead's Central Bar, taken from the 1960's film 'Women in Love', featuring Glenda Jackson being propositioned.

The Central Bar, *Half Moon Lane, Gateshead, NE8 2AN*
Telephone: 0191 478 2543 • E-mail: gatesheadcentral@gmail.com

The Grey Nags Head

'The building is a wonderfully complete survival and deserves
to be cherished into the future' - *www.twsitelines.info*

A traditional Victorian pub in decor and style with stained glass windows, high ceilings and a majestic island bar in the middle of the single room. The walls are tastefully decorated and are adorned with pictures, bric-a-brac and local curiosities from Gateshead history. These 'beautifully intricate art-deco-influenced stained glass windows to the bar and sitting room areas, however, were specially designed for the building (as specified on the plans), with simpler but no less elegant metal fenestration to the upper floor'. Outside, the biggest impact is given by the broad rounded corner – 'a most unusual feature – with its delightful crow steps (corbie steps) hopping lightly up the gable'.

The Grey Nags Head, 227-229 High St, Gateshead NE8 1AS
Telephone: (0191) 477 1955

The Metropole

A split-level single room with bar counter at the far corner. The old layout and woodwork including original bar counter dating back to its days as a late Victorian theatre bar have sadly been removed.

Sitelines (www.twsitelines.info) tells us:

'This three-storey public house was originally part of the larger Metropole Theatre building, erected [in 1896] to great fanfare at the end of the 19th century by Weldon Watts. The building was lauded in the press at the time, and hoped to encourage High Street improvements… The stalls entrance from the building's time as a cinema is still visible to the East elevation with a cast iron supporting pillar and 'Scala' inlaid into the floor. The corner site at the heart of Gateshead coupled with the highly ornamented style creates an imposing presence and expresses the theatrical history of the building'.

The Metropole,
262 High Street,
Gateshead, NE8 1EL
Telephone:
01914 776475
Facebook:
www.facebook.com/
metropolegateshead

The Queen's Head

One of the top-drawer Gateshead establishments, at the bottom of Bottle Bank. It was often in the local press due to its clientele. Here is an example:

1849 August 6.

Sir Robert Peel, bart., accompanied by his family, arrived in Newcastle, on his way to the Highlands, and stayed for the night at the Queen's Head Inn. In the course of the evening the right honourable baronet took a walk through the town, taking particular notice of Mr. Grainger's erections, the High Level Bridge, &c. He was loudly cheered by a large crowd at the railway station on his departure.

The Schooner

Originally the Ship Inn. From the website: "an independent free house run by a little baldy fella, his wife and a few other friendly folk". The pub was up and running by the early nineteenth century, as the Ship, looking out over the Tyne and for most of its history in the midst of a heavily industrialised area. Now, with industry and shipping gone, it's almost rural in its leafy environs.

The Schooner, South Shore Road, Gateshead NE8 3AF
Telephone: 0191 4777404 • Email: admin@theschooner.co.uk

Station East

Previously a railway station built on the curving viaduct approach to the High Level Bridge c. 1885-6. Replaced the Greenesfield Station for passenger traffic. Designed by John Dobson. Site of railway station on the Newcastle and Berwick Railway, opened in 1849, closed in 1965. Tripadvisor reveals that Station East was:

'Voted CAMRA Pub of the Year 2020 for Gateshead. Located on the south side of the River Tyne in Gateshead at the end of the Tyne and High-Level Bridges, Station East is a quirky space incorporating beautiful natural stonework that had previously been hidden for many years, and brings into use railway arches at the back of the pub. Stonework and steel give a natural, unpretentious industrial feel creating an atmospheric setting and drinks space'.

'It is possible to go through the main bar into a railway arch in its original condition, a must for railway buffs'.

www.pubsgalore.co.uk adds:

'Formerly the Station Hotel and now rebadged as the Station East after been [sic] bought by Hadrian and Border Brewery. This is Hadrian and Border's first flagship pub and the building has gone through a major refurbishment, with a lot of structural work to support the railway embankment that was due to collapse into the pub. This also revealed the original granite wall, which is now the main feature when entering the pub, which runs from the ground to first floor with an impressive round circular stone portal built into the wall'.

This much enlarged pub is on the site of the former Gateshead East Station and Railway Hotel. Formerly just a small pub, it is now open and spacious. There is a pleasant mezzanine floor above the main room and a further arched room to the rear below another railway bridge [whatpub.com].

The Newcastle Chronicle described it as 'a little gem tucked under the railway bridge in Hills Street at the end of the High Level Bridge'.

www.disused-stations.org.uk provides some interesting detail:

Date opened: 30.8.1850 South end of High Level Bridge; adjoins Wellington Street. Company on opening: York, Newcastle & Berwick Railway

When the full 'main line' service was introduced across the High Level Bridge both of the existing Gateshead termini, Greenesfield and Redheugh, closed to passengers, and a station was provided in their stead a short distance south-east of the High Level Bridge. It took the form of a narrow island platform, squeezed between the two tracks as they curved tightly on a series of stone arches. Its facilities were limited to a small entrance block, probably on the east side, and were greatly inferior to the elegant building with a train shed that Greenesfield had possessed. In 1862 a train shed was added to the new station to provide some comfort for the passengers on the elevated, windswept platform. This is the station which would become Gateshead East when its neighbour [Gateshead West] was added in 1868.

Station East, *Hills St, Gateshead NE8 2AS • Telephone: 0191 435 3389*

The Tilley Stone

The name of these licensed premises recalls two of the coal seams from the 'Coaly Tyne' days, when there were many mines in and around Gateshead. The premises were built in two stages, for the Gateshead Industrial Co-operative Society. The older was erected in c1895–6, on the site of a short terrace, known as Vine Row. The taller of the two buildings was added in c1940.

These premises were refurbished by J D Wetherspoon in October 2011.

The Tilley Stone is living testament to the coal industry which defined Gateshead. This JD Wetherspoon pub celebrates its heritage:

'Tyneside and coal went hand in hand for centuries, with many mines in and around Gateshead. The 'Five Quarter' seam was worked at the Derwent and Gateshead Fell pits and the 'Three Quarter' at Dunston Colliery. The 'Tilley' and 'Stone' seams were also worked at Dunston. The wooden staithes at Dunston were built in 1893 for loading coal onto ships and continued to be used until the 1970s. Now restored and a listed monument, they form reputedly the largest wooden structure in Europe and a reminder of the busy days of the 'Coaly Tyne'.

According to www.whatpub.com: 'Named after two local coal mine coal seams this October 2011, stylish conversion of former retail premises; light stained wood and a flag stone floor feature well… there are also many examples of local artists' work with a mining theme on display. Very handy for Gateshead public transport interchange and walking distance from the Baltic Centre for Contemporary Art and The Sage music & arts and conference centre.

Informative photographs educating us about all of this coal history, and about one Gateshead icon include:

Coal mining in Gateshead

Coal mining arrived in Gateshead rather later than in the rest of County Durham (which is where it was, until 1888); the first recorded mention being in 1344, although coal was probably mined before this.

The pits were relatively shallow and all the work was done by hand, but as time went on, more and more coal was produced until the mid-sixteenth century when Gateshead and Whickham contained the most productive coalfields in the world. 400,000 tons were shipped from the Tyne in 1625 as compared with 35,000 tons in 1565. Only one Gateshead family appears to have made a fortune in this trade, the appropriately named Cole family. Towards the end of the seventeenth century the easily won coal seams were largely worked out and the industry moved further from the river in search of fresh reserves at Tanfield and Stella. However, small groups of men continued to work the outcrops which larger concerns would have found uneconomic. The number of these smaller pits grew, and in 1720 there were 156 on the Shipcote Estate alone.

The New Tyne Bridge

One of the earliest Gateshead bridges to be documented was in the late 12th century. This bridge used stone arches with huge piers built on the site of a previous Roman bridge and was a joint enterprise between Newcastle and the Bishop of Durham, and the Bishop's arms appeared on a tower at the Gateshead (in County Durham) end of the bridge. Towers with gates and a drawbridge and portcullis reflected the bridge's military significance and a chapel was a feature not unusual for the times. A prison was also incorporated and several shops and houses, particularly at the Gateshead end, completed its picturesque appearance.

The upkeep of the bridge was divided between the town of Newcastle and the Prince Bishops of Durham, and boundary stones marked their limits of responsibility. Rivalry between the town and the Bishops caused friction on occasions. Newcastle eventually controlled six arches to the Bishop's four.

The idea for a bridge at the location of the present Tyne Bridge dates back to 1864, due to concern about the cost of tolls on the High Level Bridge – although the first serious discussions took place in 1883. Committees met over the next three decades, but it wasn't until the early 1920s that proposals were commenced in earnest, boosted by the chance to secure central government funding. In 29 April 1924, Newcastle and Gateshead approved the plans, and the Newcastle upon Tyne and Gateshead (Corporations) Bridge Act was passed on 7 August that year, with an estimated cost of £1 million including land acquisitions.

The completed bridge was opened on 10 October by King George V and Queen Mary, who were the first to use the roadway travelling in their Ascot landau.

The Tilley Stone, Unit 9–10 Jackson Street, Gateshead NE8 1EE
Telephone: 0191 478 0060 • E-mail: p6132@jdwetherspoon.co.uk
Website: jdwetherspoon.com/pubs/all-pubs/england/...

PUBS AROUND NEWCASTLE

The Beehive
Whitley Bay

Offers views of St. Mary's Island and the golden Long Sands of Whitley Bay. The Beehive also has a one-acre secret garden. The Grade II-listed building was built in the 18th Century and became an inn in 1896.

The Beehive, Hartley Lane, Earsdon, Whitley Bay. NE25 0SZ
Telephone: 0191 252 9352

The Brandling Arms
Gosforth

Originally built in the 1920s, The Brandling Arms is located in what is thought to have once been the stable houses for the Brandlings, a wealthy family of merchants and land and coal owners from Newcastle upon Tyne. Formerly a rectory, it stood where the western edge of the Sage now is. It was acquired by Duncan & Daglish at the turn of the 20th century and later became a Bass pub. There were alterations in 1978 when the bar and lounge were knocked through to create one big room with a massive 52-foot bar counter.

The Brandling Arms pub has its own local edition of *My Monopoly*, using Gosforth locations. Other pubs on Gosforth High Street are the Gosforth Hotel, the Queen Victoria (known once as the Northern Lights), the Blacksmith's Arms, Barca (formally Earl Grey) and the Job Bulman, a branch of Wetherspoons located in the former 1920s post office building on St Nicholas Avenue, and named after the founder of Bulman Village. The County Hotel, towards the southern end of the centre of Gosforth, is the southernmost High Street pub, famed for its extensive selection of real ale. Former public houses in Gosforth include the Collingwood in Regent Farm, and the Royal George in Brunton Park which closed in June 2009. The Three Mile Inn, which includes Scalini's Italian restaurant, is north of the High Street on the historic Great North Road (A1).

This, and the following entry, remembers the Brandling family. London born Sir John Brandling settled in Newcastle after marrying Margaret Clavering, of Callalay Castle, in Northumberland and served as sheriff in 1505 before becoming lord mayor more than once.

The name also lives on in Gosforth's Brandling Park and Brandling Village in Jesmond. It was the disastrous explosion at the Brandling-owned Felling Colliery in Gateshead in 1812 that led to the invention of the miners' safety lamp.

Most of the Brandling family were decent people, but some were corrupt businessmen, or worse - one 16th century Brandling was excommunicated after being charged with adultery, assault and other offences. He was fined £3,000 plus costs and received a prison sentence. Somehow, he neither paid the fine and nor served his time. By 1852 the family was bankrupt.

Adapted from www.thefreelibrary.com/Bangers+and+match.-a0216344807

South Gosforth has three pubs: The Millstone on Haddricksmill Road; the Brandling Villa at the corner of Haddricksmill Road and Station Road; and The Victory on Killingworth Road.

https://www.fanzo. com/en/bar/16474/ brandling-arms

*The Brandling Arms, High St., Gosforth, Newcastle-Upon-Tyne NE3 1HD
Website: www.thebrandlingarmsgosforth.co.uk*

The Brandling Villa
Gosforth

The Brandling Villa Hotel was built in 1900-1903 for W. B. Reid and Company, to the designs of Arthur Stockwell. The sandstone exterior could easily pass as a diminutive baroque town hall with its balcony, decorative finials and gablets (a small ornamental gable over a buttress or similar feature).

Gosforth gets its name from "Goose Ford" and refers to an incident that occurred when the Romans reached here in AD 55. The local people bred geese on the nearby river Ouseburn: Roman soldiers seized them all for cooking at the point about 1km north of here where the road crosses the river.

The Brandling Villa, Haddricks Mill Road, South Gosforth, Newcastle upon Tyne NE3 1QL • Telephone: 0191 284 0490
E-mail: info@brandlingvilla.co.uk • Website: www.brandlingvilla.co.uk/

The Collingwood (The Colly)
Jesmond

As we have noted, the early 1800s saw Brandling Village built for the workers of the Jesmond coal mines. The village consisted of two rows of terraced cottages either side of the long gone High Street. Soon, more substantial homes for the gentry were built on Brandling Park to the west and south. The Collingwood Arms was added to the east end of the High Street in 1836.

Robert Hewlitt, the first landlord, had a keen interest in naval history and so named the pub after the locally born Lord Collingwood (1750 – 1810) who was Commander in Chief of the British fleet in the Mediterranean and Nelson's second in command at the battle of Trafalgar. There is a claim that the pub was actually built in the shape of a ship's helm to play on this naval connection and when you look at the balcony to the east end of the building you can perhaps see why.

Robert Hewlitt left The Collingwood Arms in 1850 and the bar fell into disrepair until 1878 when a Daniel Martin took up the helm and steered the pub into the 20th Century. The terraced miners' cottages and the original Brandling Arms were demolished in the 1930s, but the Collingwood Arms survived. The

Brandling Arms was then rebuilt on the same site as its predecessor; the land between the two pubs has been a car park ever since.

In 1956 W B Reid & Co were taken over by Scottish Brewers who then went on to merge with Newcastle Breweries in 1960 and that's how The Collingwood Arms became a Scottish & Newcastle managed house.

Vice Admiral Cuthbert Collingwood, 1st Baron Collingwood (1748 –1810) is famous as second in command to Lord Nelson in several of the British victories of the Napoleonic Wars, and frequently as Nelson's successor in commands. Collingwood was born in Newcastle upon Tyne and attended the Royal Grammar School, Newcastle. At the age of twelve, he went to sea as a volunteer on board the frigate *HMS Shannon* under the command of his cousin Captain Richard Brathwaite (or Braithwaite), who looked after his nautical education. Collingwood was an unassuming, measured man: his memorial describes him as *'a typical north countryman, never duly elated by success or depressed by failure, caring little for public applause'* – a description which belies his obvious seamanship and naval success. In 1774, he sailed with *HMS Preston* to serve in the American War of Independence. The next year, following the Battle of Bunker Hill, he was promoted to lieutenant. In 1777, whilst aboard *HMS Lowestoffe*, Collingwood met Horatio Nelson for the first time, also a lieutenant. The two men formed a close bond as they moved up the ranks together. Horatio was always one step ahead however, and Collingwood would take over the command of Nelson's vessels whenever his friend was promoted. Between 1783 and 1786, they patrolled the West Indies together, seizing American ships trading illegally with the British colonies. 1797 the Battle of Cape Vincent saw Collingwood on *HMS Excellent* establishing his fighting credentials.

The Collingwood Monument stands in his honour and overlooks the River Tyne at Tynemouth. The four cannons on the walls flanking the steps at its base came from his flagship, *Royal Sovereign*. It is inscribed with Nelson's words at Trafalgar: 'See how that noble fellow Collingwood carries his ship into battle'. Towards the end of his life Collingwood would walk through his estate at Morpeth planting acorns at appropriate spots to ensure that the Royal Navy never ran out of timber for their vessels. He is buried alongside Nelson in St Paul's Cathedral.

The Collingwood Arms, Brandling Village, Jesmond, Newcastle upon Tyne NE2 4RS
Telephone: +44 1912810570 • E-mail: thecollingwoodarms@gmail.com
Website: thecollingwoodarmsjesmond.com

The County,
Gosforth

The building was listed in 1987, but life really started for it in 1826 when it was a private dwelling for the then notorious Bulman family. They were landowners and some say extortioners; by common consent they were much feared in this area – a northern Kray gang. The website tells us that in 1866 the building was converted into a pub with four bars by its new owner James Stark. He sold out to James Deucher in 1881 who went on to become a successful brewer and pub developer with public houses in Glasgow, Melrose, and the Newcastle area.

Modern Gosforth straddles the Great North Road (Gosforth High Street); it originated from 1826 as a settlement known for several decades as Bulman Village. It originally consisted of a number of properties large enough to qualify occupiers for the franchise – so-called 'forty shilling freeholders' built by the Bulman family in an attempt to bribe voters to support them in the 1826 elections. A stone bearing the name 'Bulman Village' survives and was incorporated in the façade of a later building, the Halifax Bank building north of the Brandling Arms public house. The Blacksmith's Arms public house on High Street stands on the site of the original blacksmith's forge. In 1902 Gosforth was linked by tram to Wallsend, and to Newcastle in the following year.

Inside the county

The Dr Syntax,
Prudhoe

A delightfully named pub, one of many called after racehorses. A smaller pub in nearby New Ridley, Stocksfield, is the original Doctor Syntax pub. As noted, this main road mock Tudor building built around 1915 celebrates Dr Syntax (the horse), 1811-1838; trained in Yorkshire, and raced exclusively in the North of England, Doctor Syntax won at least thirty-six races in ten seasons from 1814 to 1823. He was noted for his consistency and durability and recorded multiple wins in many of the period's leading staying races. He won the Preston Gold Cup on a record seven consecutive occasions, as well as five Lancaster Gold Cups and five Richmond Gold Cups. He was retired to stud in 1824; he was sire of Bee's Wing.

The impressive architecture and signage that is the Dr Syntax –
great name, great history, great sign.

Dr Syntax (not the horse) was a comic character dreamed up by the eighteenth-century caricaturist Thomas Rowlandson (1756-1827) who was largely employed by Rudolph Ackermann, the art publisher; he, in 1809, published in his *Poetical Magazine* The Schoolmaster's Tour—a series of plates with illustrative verses by Dr. William Combe. They were the most popular of the artist's works. This was followed by *Tour of Dr Syntax in Search of the Picturesque* which were in a 5th edition by 1813. In 1820 he published *Dr Syntax in Search of Consolation*, and in 1821 the *Third Tour of Dr Syntax in Search of a Wife*. Rowlandson also produced highly explicit erotica for a private clientele.

Syntax, by the way, is a term used in grammar to denote the correct order of words in a sentence.

Image from page 27 of The Tour of Doctor Syntax: in search of the picturesque... Fifth edition, with new plates., by William Combe. Original held and digitised by the British Library.

The Dr Syntax, 1 West Rd, Prudhoe NE42 6HP
Telephone: 01661 832004 • E-mail: info@drsyntaxprudhoe.co.uk
Website: www.drsyntaxprudhoe.co.uk/index

The Gosforth Hotel,
Gosforth

Salters Road/Gosforth High Street corner. 'The Gosforth Hotel is one of Gosforth's oldest pubs and has served as an important stopping point on the Great North Road since the 19th Century. This attractive and well-designed two storey stone building still retains many of its original features. It was constructed in 1878 with a buffet bar being added in 1891. In 1900 the property was bought by Arthur's Hill Brewery. The exceptional tiled façade was added in 1913' [www.twsitelines.info].

The Gosforth Hotel, High Street, Gosforth Newcastle Upon Tyne, NE3 1HQ
Telephone: 0191 285 6617 • E-mail: gosforth@stonegatepubs.com
Website: www.gosforthhotelnewcastle.co.uk/

The Job Bulman,
Gosforth

This former post office was built in 1928 and served Gosforth and district as general post office and sorting rooms for more than 50 years. The pub is now a Wetherspoons. The premises are now named after a respected doctor who assisted in the early development of Gosforth. In 1796, Gateshead doctor Job Bulman returned from India having made his fortune and built Coxlodge Hall for his home. He also sold plots of land along High Street to build the cottages which became known as Bulman Village. These were at first known as 'The Buildings' and stood in the area which could be regarded as the centre of modern-day Gosforth. The stable block (now offices) of Coxlodge Hall survive along with the hall's old lodge house. The hall itself was rebuilt in 1877 and demolished in 1936.

Around 1830 the name Bulman Village was cut in stone on a house at the south west corner of North Cross Street. The village name was officially changed

to Gosforth in 1878, but the original name was used, unofficially, until the World War I. Older residents continued to refer to the 'Village' well into the 20th century.

Inside the Job Bulman

The Job Bulman, *St Nicholas Avenue, Gosforth, Newcastle upon Tyne, Tyne and Wear, NE3 1AA*

The Keelman and Big Lamp Brewery,
Newburn

A pub and microbrewery on the Hadrian's Wall cross country walk. The Keelman Pub remembers the former River Tyne boatmen, immortalised in songs such as "The Keel Row" and "Cushy Butterfield"; the Keelmen transported coal up and down the river. Fine ales are brewed in the traditional way in the Big Lamp Brewery next door.

The story of the Keelman all starts with The Newburn Water Pumping Station which was built in 1854 on a part of the site of the Battle of Newburn. It housed a beam engine which was to be used to extract water from the River Tyne through a gravel filled channel for drinking, brewing and general use by the people of Newcastle. Unfortunately, the supply was less than clean, subject as it was to ingress of salt from the tides; when the channel silted up it made pumping impossible at times. The Station was soon abandoned, and the engines were moved to Wylam, where a replacement pump house still stands.

The Newburn Water Pumping Station was used as a works depot during the first half of the 20th century, but was ruinous by 1996. The Pumping Station was however protected as a grade two listed building. There followed a careful disassembly and reconstruction of the Boiler House into the Keelman Public House and the conversion of the Engine House into the Big Lamp Brewery.

The Newburn pumping engine was first installed at Elswick but the development of a sewage system made

the river water unsuitable for domestic purposes. Water pumped from the Lower Tyne was a suspected cause of the 1853 Cholera epidemic and 1527 deaths. The engine was consequently adapted and moved to Newburn in 1854. Rapidly increasing demand necessitated the construction of a second brick built pumping station at Newburn which housed two engines. Although not used after 1867 the Hawthorn engine remained in the Newburn engine house until 1913, and was eventually dumped at the bottom of a disused mine shaft in Newburn.

Adapted from *www.biglampbrewers.co.uk/keelman-pub/history-keelman-pub/*

Big Lamp is the area defined by the junction of Westgate Road and Elswick Road. A large lamp once stood here, which was reputedly one of the city's early electric street lights. Its column stood opposite the Bay Horse pub and the end of Summerhill Street. It was erected before 1900 and although it has been gone for many years it was such a prominent landmark that this spot is still called 'the big lamp'.

Quite coincidently, in 1879, Mosley Street in Newcastle had become the world's first public road to be lit by the incandescent light bulb, invented by Joseph Swan.

The Keelman and Big Lamp Brewery, *Grange Rd, Newburn, Newcastle upon Tyne NE15 8NL • Telephone: 0191 267 7766*

THE GUEST PUB:
The Dun Cow,
High Street, Sunderland

I'm only too aware that in choosing this particular pub as our guest pub we are treading on dangerous ground, encroaching as we are on Mackem territory. Nevertheless, this excellent pub is worth the foray into Wearside as it is a hostelry which would grace any city or town, even this Mackem city.

Let's let the website do the talking - pubculture.com/duncow/

This wonderfully ornate, grade 2 listed 'Edwardian Gin Palace' designed in 1901 for Robert Deuchars by the somewhat eccentric architect Benjamin F Simpson, has a remarkable exterior that features decorative creatures including a cow, lizard, cat and frog, finished off with its crowning glory – the copper domed tower, with two clocks facing the distinct and complementing crown of the Sunderland Empire, both towering landmarks of the city for over a century.

Take a step back in time as you enter the Dun Cow, listed in the national inventory of historic pub interiors. The bar of this extraordinary building has etched panels, bevelled mirrors, fine plasterwork and grand fireplaces. Chosen as the National Winner in the 2015 pub design awards and described as having 'one of the most stunning bar-backs in Britain', the Dun Cow is a perfect example of everything that a traditional British public house should be.

We welcome customers from all walks of life – city shoppers to leaders of commerce, theatre goers to retired glass blowers…the Dun Cow is a place where opinions and ideas can be shared in the company of like-minded friends.

The Dun Cow, 9 High St W, Sunderland SR1 3HA • Telephone: 0191 567 2262

SOME PUBS WE HAVE LOST –
A SELECTION

Balmbra's,
Cloth Market

The historic Cloth Market bar Balmbra's is being refurbished and transformed, phoenix-like, with support from The National Lottery Heritage Fund: the frontage will be restored and signage will be replaced with a reproduction of the original from the 1900s.

Balmbra's in the 1950s

John Balmbra pronounced his venue as one of the most premium venues in the city, selling 'highly-flavoured wines, foreign and British spirits, fine sparkling English and Scotch Ales, London and Dublin stout. An excellent Skittle Ground is being fit up. Good Stabling, &c.' - *The Newcastle Courant*, 27th of November 1840.'

Immortalised in the iconic song *The Blaydon Races*, Balmbra's is where the famous song was first performed in June, 1862 by its creator, George Geordie Ridley, the renowned Gateshead-born singer and songwriter (whose other notable musical composition was the rousing *Cushy Butterfield*): "I took the bus from Balmbra's/ And she was heavy laden/ Away we went along Collingwood Street/ That's on the Road to Blaydon."

By May 1850 the room was being reported on as Balmbra's Music Saloon, the *ERA* carried the following report in their 19th of May 1850 edition saying: 'Mr. Balmbra's Music Saloon - This popular establishment continues to increase in attraction…' The building would later become known as Balmbra's Music Hall, but would eventually be renamed the Royal Music Hall in 1859, and then the Wheatsheaf Music Hall in 1864. After a 1902 refit it was renamed the Carlton Hotel and brewers Steel, Coulson & Co Ltd of Edinburgh took over the tenancy.

Balmbra's was then a hugely popular music hall and pub – probably the most famous outside London. After more alterations in 1955 it was used as a billiard hall but became a music hall again in 1962 as Balmbra's. It was damaged by a fire in 2014 during its time as 'Balmbra's Motown Bar', largely destroying the interior of the building. Three bay windows will be reopened and one of the most famous parts of Balmbra's, the barrel-vaulted roof, is being preserved.

The Malhotra leisure group, which also owns the Three Mile in Gosforth, Leila Lily's and the Grey Street Hotel, is creating a pop-up bar to bring the building back into public use and generate some income as a stop gap until the wider transformation and redevelopment of the site can be carried out in the future.

The Newcastle Chronicle takes up the story:

The story of the famous venue began in the midst of Tyneside's Victorian era when John Balmbra became licensee of the Wheatsheaf Inn in the Cloth Market in 1858, and the inn adopted its now-famous name. At that time, the more competitive licensees in Newcastle offered entertainment to pull in the crowds. Balmbra went one step further and opened a full-scale music hall behind his premises. In 1864 when Balmbra died, the next landlord [Thomas Handford (1835-1876) and his elder brother, Henry (1829-1888), blackface artistes] introduced a regular charge for seats and added an extra entrance down the side as business boomed.

Handford took over on New Years Day 1864 and, by way of honouring his friend, he re-branded the Wheatsheaf as Balmbra's Music Hall. But purpose-built variety theatres were opening, and by the end of the 19th century the Wheatsheaf was, once again, a normal public house. The name was changed to the Carlton and, despite alterations being made to the building in 1956, it had become little more than a licensed billiard hall. *The Chronicle* concludes:

Revived, however in 1962, to coincide with the centenary of the Blaydon Races, the brewery converted the Carlton back to its original music hall form, and revived the name Balmbra's.

…And reminds us that the Blaydon Races (the horse races that is, as celebrated in the eponymous song first aired at Balmbra's 160 or so years ago) were last run at Stella Haugh on the south bank of the Tyne in 1916. Another lost pub…

BLAYDON RACES

I WENT TO BLAYDON RACES
'TWAS ON THE 9TH OF JUNE
EIGHTEEN HUNDRED AND SIXTY TWO
ON A SUMMER'S AFTERNOON
WE TOOK THE BUS FROM BALMBRAS
AND SHE WAS HEAVY LADEN
AWAY WE WENT ALONG COLLINGWOOD STREET
THAT'S ON THE ROAD TO BLAYDON

OH ME LADS
YOU SHOULD'VE SEEN US GANNIN'
PASSING THE FOLKS ALONG THE ROAD
JUST AS THEY WERE STANNIN'
ALL THE LADS AND LASSES THERE
ALL WITH' SMILIN FACES
GANNIN ALONG THE SCOTSWOOD ROAD
TO SEE THE BLAYDON RACES

—— TOON ARMY ——

The Chain Locker,
North Shields

The Chain Locker was situated on New Quay, North Shields at the entrance to the ferry. It was previously known as the Crane House Vaults and has now been converted to apartments. The pub is in the New Quay conservation area next to the listed Collingwood Mansions and the former Northumberland Arms pub. The building you see today went up in 1905. There has been a brewery or inn on the site since the days when stagecoaches took ships' passengers to and from Newcastle when the tide prevented sailing upriver.

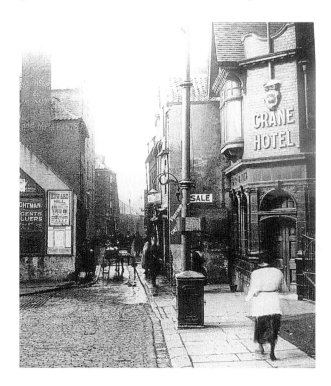

Originally a malting house, the building became a pub in 1904 and was known as the Crane House Vaults until renamed The Chain Locker in 1986. But there has been a pub here since at least 1850 when it was also called the Crane House Vaults after a dockside crane and was part of the Newcastle Breweries estate; they owned 28 of the Borough of Tynemouth's 207 pubs in 1892. Competition came from the Duke of Cumberland (landowner, not the pub) who owned thirteen. The Chain Locker/Crane House was actually the last building in Duke Street where five of the 50 numbered buildings were pubs and one was the High Brewery which served, along with Tyne Brewery, Newcastle Breweries after 1890, their barrels shipped between the two by a boat appropriately named *The Brewer*.

The pub was rebuilt in 1905 in the style reminiscent of Arts and Crafts architect Norman Shaw with its large oriel window on the east façade. The ground floor, though, is Edwardian, faced as it is in glazed faience.

www.twsitelines.info fills in some details:

A property known as the "Crane House" is listed in records from 1833 onwards at 44 Duke Street, 2 New Quay, 2 Duke Street and 50 Duke Street. It was owned by Mrs Ann Kirby until she died in 1837 or 1838. The house at the rear was called Kirby's House built onto Kirby's Bank. The properties were listed as houses, shops and pubs. They passed into the hands of W.H. Allison and Co., who operated a brewery in one of the buildings, and went on in 1890 to form the Newcastle Breweries with four other brewery companies. By 1880 the collection of buildings on Duke Street consisted of The Crane House, with a small maltings to the rear, and the adjoining Crown and Thistle pub with stables to the rear. Next to this were warehouses and cottages. In 1905 the Crane House and malting was demolished and rebuilt set back from the road by Joseph Oswald and Son.

The Crown & Sceptre,
Newcastle

The Crown & Sceptre was in High Friar Street; it is remembered for being one of the two pubs Irishman Will Curley (real name Cawley) invested in using his earnings from a boxing career which included a World Featherweight Title final in 1899 which he lost on points in New York. The other pub was on Gateshead High Street, the Phoenix; both, as to be expected, were nicknamed Curley's. Curley was in the trade for 50 years and put money into St James Hall which became the city's premier boxing venue. The Crown & Sceptre closed in the early 1970s.

The Goat, Bottle Bank,
Gateshead

F amous for the carved entrance; it now grazes in the Shipley Art Gallery. The Goat was once the Navries, the Bell of the Hoop (1616) and the Spread Eagle (1627).

The Court of Justice was held for many years in the long room, from where prisoners were sent to Durham Gaol. Here also was the distribution by the wardens of St. Mary's of the various charities. After a parade on November 16th 1803, the colours of the first Gateshead Volunteers, commanded by Cuthbert Ellison Esq., were deposited at the Goat Inn. They remained here until 1854 when Cuthbert Ellison presented them to Gateshead Council. The inn provided a dinner for a distinguished group of officers who had taken part in the parade, including the Right Hon. The Earl of Strathmore, Cuthbert Ellison Esq., J. Carr Esq. and others, along with the officers of Newcastle and Gateshead Volunteers. It was demolished to make way for the New Tyne Bridge [in 1925].

The Goat, the pub that is, has a long and illustrious history as recounted by Sitelines [www. twsitelines.info]

150

The Golden Fleece/Porthole,
North Shields

The 1897 built Golden Fleece stands on the site of an 1850s pub. Deuchars bought the pub and rebuilt it in August 1897 adding touches of idiosyncrasy. The terracotta and red brick exterior is remarkably well-preserved – the only significant change over the decades being the new name in the 1980s.

The designers of the building were theatre designers, Frank Matcham, as reflected in the decorative treatment, especially the first floor balcony which resembles a theatre box. The Porthole closed in 2013.

The Green Tree,
Old Benwell

Another pub with boxing associations – it was extended in 1930 and lasted out until the '90s. In its last years local boxer John Davison – a former WBC international featherweight champion in 1990 ran 'boxercise' classes there.

The Half Moon,
Bigg Market

The Half Moon was in the Grade II Half Moon Chambers in the Bigg Market in Newcastle. Inscribed above the doors is: "BUILT AD 1550 / REBUILT AD 1905". The magnificent façade survives more or less as commissioned by Archibald Arrol & Sons Ltd of Alloa, indicative of the Scottish brewery invasion of the late 19th century. The pub was also the headquarters of brewers Meikle & Deuchars; subsequently Robert Deuchar & Co Ltd amassed a large estate of tied houses before being taken over by Newcastle Breweries Ltd in 1953. The 1905 rebuild shows the influence of Charles Rennie Mackintosh with its five storey Art Nouveau façade. The stone crescent moon in the niche in the uppermost part of the central scrolled gable has since disappeared.

History remembers the Half Moon in Mackenzie's 1827 history of Newcastle as 'the resort of many respectable farmers on market days'. In Get Carter, the original Vic and Comet doubled for the interior of the Half Moon – with either side of the horsehoe bar being used for two different, but equally important, Michael Caine scenes.

The Hawks' Arms,
Gateshead

As we have noted, the Hawks' Arms at 50 East Street in Gateshead remembers the Hawks family (c.1750 – 1889) - one of the most powerful British industrial dynasties of the Industrial Revolution. The Hawks owned several companies in northern England and in the City of London (including Hawks and Co., Hawks, Crawshay, and Stanley, and Hawks, Crawshay and Sons) all of which were big in iron manufacture and engineering, which they exported worldwide using their own ships. The Crawshay pub, was at no. 22 East Street patronised by workers from John Abbot and Co of Park Iron Works, Gateshead, iron founders and steam and hydraulic engineers.

The Hawks family were involved in merchant banking, and in freemasonry, and in Whig free-trade politics. They developed areas of West London, including Pembroke Square, Kensington.

The Hawks employed over 2000 people and enjoyed a global reputation for engineering and bridge-building. Their Gateshead factories were called New Deptford and New Woolwich after the location of two of its warehouses on the River Thames. The company built the High Level Bridge across the River Tyne that was opened by Queen Victoria in 1849; and numerous bridges including in Constantinople and India; and lighthouses in France; and ironclad warships and materials for the Royal Navy during the Napoleonic Wars; and large contracts for the East India Company. The Hawks produced the first iron boat, the Vulcan, in 1821. Famous family members included Sir Robert Shafto Hawks (1768 - 1840).

The Tynemouth poet Joseph Skipsey (the Pitman Poet) worked for the Hawks' Gateshead ironworks, from 1859 to 1863, until one of his children was killed in an accident at the works in 1863. His first volume of poetry was published in Durham in 1858, a copy of which came to the attention of James Thomas Clephan, at that time editor of the *Gateshead Observer*, a relatively new newspaper and the first in Gateshead. When told by Skipsey of his dire straits, Clephan got him a job at Hawks, Crawshay and Sons ironworks in Gateshead.

The Hawks' Arms had a nickname – 'Black Tom' after Thomas Hunter, landlord in the 1880s.

The Lord Chancellor/Maceys,
31 Groat Market

Former names for Maceys are the Lord Chancellor, Cosy Joes, Pop & Rewind. Late eighteenth century or early nineteenth century; after the interior refurbishment – 'the real attraction of the pub' (Pearson p. 15) - it comprises 'a complex arrangement of rooms and screens' and was called the Lord Chancellor in 1896. Unusually, 'the rear select bar was divided by screens into three distinct areas with snob screens on the counter preventing customers from seeing into adjacent parts of the bar, and the publican from observing the customers'. This six-roomed renovation broke new ground in Newcastle where pubs generally consisted of a long bar and no screens; long bars were criticised when the Clerk to the Justices for Newcastle reported to the Royal Commission on the Liquor Licensing Laws that they 'unduly encouraged drinking'. Whatever next in a pub? He suggested 'that men would enter a pub and instead of having a drink or two in a well screened bar and then leaving, would be able to see their friends in all parts of the pub and would therefore feel forced to buy extra rounds of drinks (Pearson p. 15).

The famous white horse

154

Ridley Court separated it from the White Horse Inn, famous for its three dimensional white horse pub sign facing out into Groat Market. Elizabeth Davison (an unmarried Glaswegian lady) was the tenant in the early 1870s followed a decade later by Mr and Mrs Elsbury; the pub was taken over by wine and spirit merchants S. Oliver & Co in 1892.

The Lord Chancellor was remodelled in 1928 under the tenancy of brewers Robinson & Anderson when the screens were tragically removed to make way for an extension of the public bar - and again in 1950. In 1948 Robinson & Anderson were taken over by Bradford brewers Hammonds United Breweries Ltd who became part of Northern Breweries Ltd in 1959. In 1985 it became Maceys, in the 1990s allegedly a haunt of Newcastle United footballers. There is also a story that a man was blasted to death inside the packed pub and another man was also shot.

The Lord Hill

As everywhere, the public house played an important role in local football with a pint or two before and after the game – a crucial part of the match day experience for many – win or lose. Newcastle is no exception. In the 1880s and 1890s things football wise were not as simple as they are today: back then the two top local teams were Newcastle East End and Newcastle West End. West End eventually ended up playing at St James' Park changing at the Lord Hill nearby on Barrack Road. Licensee John Black eventually became a director of Newcastle United. East End, meanwhile, issued a share offer and those who invested included brewer Robert Deuchar and his son Farquhar as well as the

licensees of the Gosforth Hotel, the Chester in Shieldfield, the Glendale (Byker) and the Northumberland Arms. Merger came in 1892 to form Newcastle United playing at St James' Park.

The Black Bull, the Duke of Wellington, the Windsor Hotel, and the Bay Horse on Barrack Road would also have played host to United fans in the club's early years.

The Lord Hill was demolished in the 1960s to be replaced by the Magpie Club, later to become a Newcastle United supporters private social club, before it was demolished. Student accommodation now occupies the site. For the 1980-1981 season £100,000 saw a deal go through with Scottish & Newcastle sponsoring the distinctive shirts of the Magpies. Greenalls took over only for Scottish and Newcastle to come back for a second stint. Newcastle Brown Ale has also featured as sponsors.

The Old Robin Hood Inn,
Pilgrim Street

I n the late 19th century, it was not uncommon for the police to raid pubs, for a number of reasons. In 1870 the Old Robin Hood was unexpected hosts of the Newcastle constabulary. The *Newcastle Courant* of July 22, 1870 reported how Adam Edmonds was in the dock for selling imported wines without a licence. He was joined by Isabella Ford of Dog Bank, Joshua Greenwell of Oyster Shell Lane, Joseph Westmoreland of the Fighting Cocks Inn and two others. An excise officer had visited the homes of each of them to purchase a glass of port or sherry. They offered foreign wines for which they had no licence and were each fined £5.00 each.

There it is to the right of the dray.

157

The Ship Inn,
Gateshead

The Turk's Head,
Grey Street

Kathleen Brown was one of Newcastle's suffragettes. After she was arrested for throwing stones in Whitehall, Brown was sentenced to seven days solitary confinement at Holloway Prison, where she went on hunger strike. On her release, in July 1909, a large group of supporters met her at Newcastle Central Station, bearing banners and carriages decorated in the suffragette colours of white, green and purple. Following a celebratory tea at the Turks Head Hotel, she delivered a speech to a large crowd at the Haymarket. Later that year there were protests when Chancellor, Lloyd George, visited Newcastle in October. Lady Constance Lytton, Kathleen Brown, and Emily Wilding Davison, were amongst those who threw stones, in what was later referred to as "the Battle of Newcastle". Windows in the Liberal Club on Pilgrim Street were smashed and when Lloyd George's car was moving through the Haymarket, Lady Lytton threw a stone at it, to which the following message was attached: "To Lloyd-George, Rebellion Against Tyranny is Obedience to God. Deeds, not Words". At the barrier which had been erected in Percy Street, Jane Brailsford produced an axe concealed with a bunch of flowers and began hacking at the barrier.

On the 8th of March 2017, to mark International Women's Day, a heritage plaque was placed on the former Turks Head Hotel.

Grey Street was built c1835 by Richard Grainger as part of the 19th Century redevelopment of Newcastle City Centre. Nos. 69 to 73 was the former Royal Turk's Head Hotel, opposite the Theatre Royal, and popular

with theatregoers. Reputably the Beatles wrote *She Loves You* while staying at the hotel, after playing at the Majestic in 1963 as part of their tour with Roy Orbison and Gerry & The Pacemakers. Hmm. In an interview McCartney said:

> There was a Bobby Rydell song out at the time, *Forget Him* and, as often happens, you think of one song when you write another. We were in a van up in Newcastle-Upon-Tyne. I'd planned an 'answering song' where a couple of us would sing 'she loves you' and the other ones would answer 'yeah yeah'.

> We decided that was a crummy idea but at least we then had the idea of a song called 'She Loves You'. So we sat in the hotel bedroom for a few hours and wrote it — John and I, sitting on twin beds with guitars.

However, in 2003, plans to install a plaque at the hotel were stalled after it turned out neither Paul McCartney nor Ringo Starr, the surviving Beatles, could recall whether it was the Imperial Hotel in Jesmond or the Royal Turk's Head where the group had stayed. In 1965 it was designated a Grade II listed building and later it was used by Barclays Bank and became known as Barclays House.

The Vine Inn, and the Unicorn Inn,
Bigg Market

Today Freemans at 1 Bigg Market is on the site of the Vine Inn which gloried in its superb interior and the quality decorative detail in its five bars by Septimus Oswald. Pearson (page 23) tells how 'the detailed joinery of the counter and the back fitting of the bar show late Victorian/Edwardian pub design at its best… the quality of its interior showed to perfection the importance of the wine and spirit merchants as pub licensees in Newcastle'.

Bigg Market in 1842; the pub in the middle is the Unicorn Inn which stood in Bigg Market from Elizabethan times to 1883. The Victoria Tunnel runs from the north of Newcastle, under the city streets, down to where the Ouseburn enters the River Tyne.

When the tunnel was finally completed on January 8, 1842, a celebratory party for two hundred workmen was held at the Unicorn Inn in Newcastle's Bigg Market.

Accounts from the time report that the thirsty workers were "regaled with a substantial supper and strong ale", and there was entertainment from the Albion Band who "enlivened the joyous occasion with their music".

Mrs Rachel Dixon, the landlady, served the ale and joined in the celebrations.

The Wolsington Hotel,
Walkergate

The Wolsington House Public House appears on Ordnance Survey first edition (1896), however the date over the door tells that this was rebuilt as the Wolsington Hotel in 1902 when it belonged to Gateshead brewer, Isaac Tucker. The pub was known locally as "Seaman Watson's" after its former manager and featherweight boxing champion "Seaman" Tommy Watson. The pub was also famous from the 1950s for Sailor, the resident South African grey parrot who was partial to cocktail cherries.

Thomas Watson (1908 –1971) was British featherweight champion between 1932 and 1934. Born in Newcastle upon Tyne, Watson served in the Royal Navy, where he was lightweight champion. For more information see Jarrett, John (1997) *Byker to Broadway: The Fighting Life and Times of Seaman Tommy Watson*, Bewick Press.

The pub was close to the Colliery Engine Inn and is made up of two terraced houses. The Wolsington was built in 1902 on the site of an earlier pub (from about 1834) of the same name as testified by a North Shields directory listed as John Veitch's alehouse. In 1899 it was bought by Andrew Nichol Dodds, innkeeper, philanthropist and local councillor and a blacksmith by trade. Dodds went on to become something of a radical, a Chartist and was one of the pioneers of the Co-operative movement. In his spare time, he showed prize-winning Bedlington terriers and homing pigeons. Dodds warmed to innkeeping and owned five in the Borough of Tynemouth and two in South Shields by 1892. In 1919 the pub was sold to W.B. Reid & Co. The Wolsington was further extended in 1929.

Pubs like the Wolsington and the Porthole had a huge market on their doorsteps: North Shields was expanding out of its industrial base into a huge fishing port; in 1909 there were 76 steam trawlers (invented in Shields) based there with others visiting; 2,600 people were employed in the local fishing industry rising to 6,000 when herring shoals were offshore bringing 600 herring boats with them.

As we have seen pubs at this time were anxious to build market share and so jazzed up their offering and their ambience. Pearson (p. 52) sees the Porthole and the Wolsington as good examples of 'turn of the century idiosyncrasy in pub design… fun architecture with a serious commercial purpose, and are certainly an important part of architectural and social history'.

https://pubsnewcastle.co.uk/MicroBrewPubs.htm • https://craftbeernewcastle.co.uk/newcastle-breweries/ https://www.tripadvisor.co.uk/Attractions-g186394-Activities-c36-t133-Newcastle_upon_Tyne_Tyne_ and_Wear_England.html

SOME NORTH EAST BREWERIES
- PAST & PRESENT

In the earliest days in the north east, as elsewhere, most inns, taverns and pubs were independent entities brewing their own beer or ale; examples in Gateshead, for example, include the Queen's Arms, the Blue Bell and the Grey Nag's Head. Then came Common Brewers, brewing on behalf of other concerns and this is how most beer was then produced. Common Brewers included the Hillgate Brewery, the Oakwellgate Brewery of McLeod and Sons, the Ellison Street Brewery and Dawson & Co's Vulcan Brewery.

As we have seen, the 1869 Wine and Beer House ignited a reaction in brewers to protect their businesses from the magistrates who were now empowered to agree to or deny licenses, and later to close pubs altogether. This obviously focused the minds of breweries to ensure that their houses or prospective houses were up to scratch and passed all the thresholds the magistrates were testing when deciding to grant or not to grant. As a result there was a slew of takeovers, buyouts, mergers and new builds through which brewers sought to build up estates.

The mobility and logistics opportunities offered by the emerging railway system facilitated this with different, hitherto alien, brews flowing in and out of specific regions like the north east where beers from Burton, London and Scotland flooded in. Agents moved in and agencies flourished within territories originally considered sacrosanct by local brewers. Local breweries expanded into to regional, national and then international concerns.

Here are a few examples of north east brewers.

John Barras & Co.,
Newcastle and Gateshead

John Barras & Co was probably the biggest player in the Newcastle Breweries consortium; Barras was a wealthy home brewer from Whickham who established a brewery in Gateshead in 1770.

In 1884 John Barras Jnr took over The Tyne Brewery and in 1890 Newcastle Breweries was established... and for a while Newcastle Brown Ale was brewed in Gateshead.

Their 40 Newcastle pubs included: Bee Hive, High Bridge; Bobby Shafto, Armstrong Road; Bourgogne's, Newgate Street; Chieftain (after the tank), Westmorland Road (opened 1967); Colliery Engine Inn, Shields Road, Walkergate; Crow's Nest Hotel, Barras Bridge; Old Custom House, Sandhill/ Quayside (closed 1926) and Ordnance Arms, Gallowgate. There were 20 in Gateshead, seven in Sunderland and ones as far away as Redcar and Billingham.

The Chieftain, of course, was manufactured at the Vickers factory on Scotswood Road. It boasted a themed interior. The actual tank used in the pub's opening promotion was from the 15th/19th King's Royal Hussars.

The company merged with Scottish Brewers Ltd. 1960 to form Scottish & Newcastle Breweries Ltd. This firm closed in 2005 with brewing transferred to the Northern Clubs Federation Brewery Ltd at Dunston.

J.W. Cameron's Lion Brewery,
(West) Hartlepool

Thanks to two artesian wells, one of them 250-foot deep, beer has been flowing in Stranton, West Hartlepool, now Hartlepool, since 1572. The Vicar of Stranton, James Lackinby, left his stepeleade (a vital brewing tool) to William Harding, Vicar of Hart, in his will. The New Burn Brewery, near Newburn Bridge, had to close because its water became contaminated. J.W. Cameron's Lion Brewery is on a site that has been occupied by breweries since 1852 when William Waldon first set up business there having bought the land and business from Ralph Walker for £300.00, near to the natural spring which ever since has provided the water for their fine beer. When Waldon died in 1854 his widow, Jane, and son took on the business and then in 1865 it and its sixteen public houses passed into the hands of an employee who went by the name of John William Cameron. Cameron assumed control of the Lion Brewery and its 16 inns and beer houses on a 21-year lease. Over those 21 years Cameron was in expansionist mode, taking over more breweries and building the Lion Brewery we see today in 1892, buying the business from the Waldon family for £34,442. Its opulence is still visible today: the floor and walls of the brew house are furnished with Italian marble that cost £7,000 in 1970.

In 1894 the company went public, valued at £345,000, and owned 119 public houses; a number of other breweries such as Lambton's of Sunderland were acquired and in 1897, T E Chapman & Son of Sunderland with 83 public houses. That same year, the Lion Brewery was further extended, to a 70 quarter capacity, capable of producing 130,000 barrels a year. In 1899 Camerons began to bottle mineral water and the company continued to expand. By this time they owned 400 licensed premises, including most of West Hartlepool's public houses. Cameron's day job was as a colonel in the 4th Durham Volunteers; he and wife Emma lived in Greenbank in Stranton. When he died in 1896 younger brother Captain Watson Cameron took over the brewery and in 1905 built a hospital in memory for the people of West Hartlepool and Hartlepool. In 1910, Heslop's Grange Brewery in Stockton was acquired along with its 28 licensed houses; 1920 saw the acquisition of Robert Newton Ltd of Newcastle with its 35 licences, and Plews and Sons Ltd of Darlington.

Cameron's memorabilia

Legendary 'Strongarm Bitter' a distinctive ruby red bitter was launched in 1955, the beer of choice for many a strong-armed shipbuilder and, later, steelworker. At 4% ABV it was developed in response to the workers' demand for a stronger pint; indeed, it was the strongest bitter in the North East and a snip at 1s 7d a pint. Total production of Strongarm surpassed one billion pints in 2000. The *2002 Good Beer Guide* remarked that Strongarm was "Now substantially improved and with consistent character". Strongarm is made with 18 per cent crystal malt, which contributes significantly to its distinctive ruby red colour and its roasted, malty flavour. The barley comes from Yorkshire and Scotland.

More takeovers followed: a controlling interest was acquired in John J Hunt, which owned the Ebor Brewery in York and Scarborough & Whitby Breweries along with 221 licensed public houses for around £400,000 in 1953. In 1956 J Fryer & Sons of Brompton-on-Swale was acquired; in 1959 the West Auckland Brewery was acquired with 80 licensed public houses and in 1961 Russell & Wrangham of Malton with 90 licensed public houses. After one hundred years of growth through brewery acquisitions, the company had an estate of 750 licensed premises throughout the North East and North Yorkshire by the 1960s.

Camerons was one of the first breweries to sponsor football kits, with Middlesbrough FC from 1984–86 and Hartlepool United from 1985-1990 and 1993-2000. In 1985, Cameron's held five per cent of the UK beer market. In 1986, Cameron's acquired 90 pubs from Mansfield Brewery, including 78 northern pubs and clubs, most of which were former North Country Breweries outlets, for £13 million. In 1988, the company expanded into the North West for the first time after it acquired 17 pubs in north Lancashire.

In 1988, Camerons and Tolly Cobbold were sold to Brent Walker for £248 million. Camerons controlled 480 licensed public houses and 270 hotels and off-licences. In 1989, Camerons Brewery was described as one of the most efficient in the country, with a total annual capacity of over 500,000 barrels and production of 400,000.

In 1991, the heavily indebted Brent Walker sold the brewery and 51 pubs to Wolverhampton & Dudley for £18.7 million. Brent Walker retained the bulk of the Cameron's estate when they inherited 101 pubs. Most customers believed that Camerons' beers greatly improved after being acquired by W&D who sold the company to Castle Eden in 2002, who in turn closed their own site, moving all production to Camerons. In 2003, £500,000 was spent on a new bottling line and a microbrewery opened; the Visitor Centre opened in 2004 in the former Stranton pub.

For the exhibition and brewery tours contact vc@cameronsbrewery.com

In 2013 Cameron's purchased the Hexham based Head of Steam cask and craft beer group along with seven pubs throughout the north; the estate now includes pubs in Newcastle, (Quayside), Gateshead, Sunderland (Dun Cow and Ship Isis), Durham, Norton, Whitby, Leeds, Hull and York. Other Tyneside pubs include The Cluny, The Cluny 2 and Tilley's and Central in Gateshead. The acquisition of Leeds Brewery came next in 2017 with their seven pubs.

The company now has a relatively small tied estate of 75 houses but is still the ninth largest brewery in the country. It is the largest independent brewer in the North East of England, with a brewery capacity of 1.5 million hectolitres (900,000 hl production in 2012). It is one of the oldest industrial concerns in Hartlepool, and has historically been one of the town's largest employers.

Derek Gardner being presented with a pint of Strongarm
by John Watson Cameron December 1967

Trussing the Cooper - *The time-honoured ceremony of 'Trussing the Cooper' is still observed to this day. On completion of a seven year apprenticeship the fledgling cooper would build a barrel and sit in it. Colleagues would then pour in soot, ash, bad beer, old grain – anything in fact that was disgusting. The barrel would then be turned on its side and rolled around the workshop. A suitably besmirched ex-apprentice would then be presented with his or her indentures, and a pint. Courtesy of and © Marie-Louise McKay, The History of the Lion Brewery.*

James Deuchar Ltd., Newcastle

James Deuchar Ltd arrived on Tyneside in the 1860s and became publican of the Argyle. He acquired the Ridley Arms Brewery, Pilgrim Street, Newcastle–upon–Tyne, in 1880. In 1887 James Deuchar started brewing at the Monkwearmouth Brewery, Sunderland, which had belonged to W H Allison & Co. The firm became a limited company in 1894. Deuchar quickly built up a large estate of North East pubs, including the Argyle, the Golden Fleece and the Grey Nag's Head.

By 1900 it had bought the Lochside Brewery of William Ross & Co, Montrose and the aerated water plant of Robert Emmerson in Scotswood Road, Newcastle. Brewing was concentrated in Montrose and the Monkwearmouth brewery was used for storage and bottling. In 1957 brewing ceased in Montrose and was moved to the old Robert Deuchar brewery in Duddingston.

Newcastle Breweries Ltd acquired the company along with 125 licensed houses and hotels, in 1956, having acquired Robert Deuchar in 1953. The Lochside Brewery stopped brewing in the same year, and it was sold to Macnab Distilleries Ltd and converted to a whisky distillery. Distilling ceased in 1992 and the building was demolished in 2005 [Source: Tyne & Wear Archives].

The company's Scottish brewed beers were delivered to Tyneside by steamer: *Lochside I* and *Lochside II.* The Lochside pub in Heaton opened just before the takeover by Newcastle Breweries.

169

Robert Deuchar Ltd.

Robert Deuchar Ltd was founded 1869 when Robert Deuchar acquired the Chancellor's Head Inn, 114 Newgate Street, leased J. S. Arnison's Sandyford Brewery c.1888 and purchased the estate after his death in 1892. Acquired Simson & McPherson Ltd of Edinburgh 1900 and all brewing was transferred to Duddingston Brewery, Edinburgh by 1920 from where stock was trained to Newcastle. Acquired by Newcastle Breweries Ltd. 1954 with 360 public houses; brewing ceased in 1961.

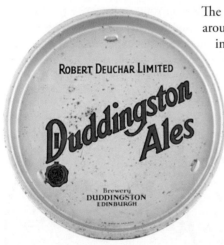

The company had 78 houses in and around Newcastle with a further thirteen in and around Gateshead including the Black Bull (Mulgrave Terrace) and the Crystal Palace. There were also six in Sunderland and one in Middlesbrough.

Newcastle Breweries Ltd.,
Tyne Brewery, Newcastle

As noted, Newcastle Breweries was a consortium of five existing breweries: John Barras & Co. Ltd, Tyne Brewery; William Henry Allison & Co, High Brewery, Duke Street, North Shields; Monkwearmouth Brewery, Sunderland; Swinburne & Co, Gateshead and Carr Brothers & Carr, Low Lights, North Shields, making a total of 215 public houses between them. The managing director was Thomas Watson Lovibond who had previously managed the Barras brewery and was chairman of the Brewers Society in 1899 and 1900.

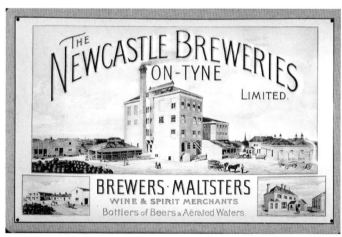

Northern Clubs Federation Brewery Ltd.

S tarted off at Alnwick in 1919 when George Stott Smart's former brewery was acquired but this was found not to be serviceable, so brewing was transferred to Hedley Street, Newcastle where brewing began in March 1921. The name changed to Northern Clubs Federation Brewery Ltd in 1926. A short lease on John Buchanan's Hanover Square Brewery was taken in 1927; the brewery moved to the Hanover Street Brewery 1931. John Buchanan pubs included the Battery Inn & Brewhouse, South Street/Forth Street, Newcastle; and the Fat Ox, Whitley Bay.

Buchanan had acquired the Hanover Square brewery in 1883. He sold fifteen houses in 1927 and leased the brewery to the Northern Clubs Federation Brewery Ltd who then exercised an option to purchase in 1929.

In 1980 Northern Clubs moved to a new brewery at Dunston in Gateshead. In 2004 they were bought by Scottish & Newcastle who had announced the closure of their Newcastle brewery. They traded as Newcastle Federation Breweries until closed in 2010 by Heineken.

J. Nimmo & Sons Ltd,
Castle Eden Brewery, Castle Eden

Castle Eden Brewery has been a feature of the north east brewery landscape since 1826 when it was founded by John Nimmo (c.1801 - 1867) who leased the Regency building from the Burdon family of Castle Eden. A contemporary description of Castle Eden village tells us that it was "2 ½ miles from the sea on the high road from Stockton to Sunderland...where there is a large and commodious inn, which is the only posting house between these two towns". This was the Commercial Inn from which the two coaches, The Royal Mail and The Pilot and Expedition, left daily. Nimmo began brewing at the Castle Eden Inn in Castle Eden, which had its own brewhouse.

The brewery

173

On the death of John Nimmo, his son, William John Nimmo (1828 - 1901) took over; between 1871 and 1888 the company prospered and the value of the fixtures at the brewery rose from £138 to £1765. A brewery deed of 1889 says that William Nimmo leased "Brewery Malt House... dwelling houses, offices and buildings which include the premises formerly occupied by county police stations as the same have been altered or adopted for brewing purposes or are in course of being so".

The Nimmo story is a story of relentless progress: in 1864 the brewery plant was remodelled; 1869 gas lighting was introduced; 1870 extensive malting completed; 1871 a bonded warehouse was built; in 1880 a private railway siding constructed; 1909 saw electric power station, pumping plant and tanks and boilers installed; in 1910 four copper fermenting vessels were added; in 1955 maltings were installed, including a Saladin Box which trebled malt output. Nimmo was the first brewers in the north east to adopt the crown cork in place of the old full cork, and the first to install beer canning equipment. Nimmo were also one of the first brewers in the country to place large storage tanks in public houses, so enabling beer to be delivered by road tanker. Nimmo was an innovative man, building the second pneumatic maltings in England in 1878-9, and his was among the first breweries to adopt powered drays in 1892.

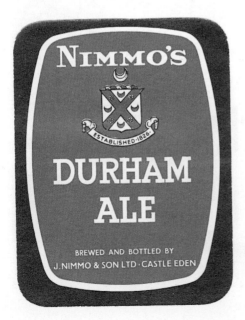

In 1892, J. Nimmo & Son Ltd was registered as a limited liability company with forty-one public houses. The company continued to go from strength to strength: innovative alterations in 1910 made Castle Eden one of the most state-of-the-art breweries in the country while output doubled between 1906 and 1914. In 1912 the company acquired the brewing business of Thomas Chilton in Seaham, including their twelve public houses. Between 1912 and 1920, production reached a record output of more than 42,000 barrels. In 1930 the properties of the Durham and North Yorkshire Public House Trust were acquired. By 1942 nearly a third of the output was in bottles and an automatic bottling plant was up and running in 1950. Under the Nimmos, the brewery grew to annual capacity of 75,000 barrels with an estate of 125 pubs. William John Nimmo II died in 1952 without any sons, so his daughter, Eileen Denton Trechman (1905 - 2004), became chair of the company; at the time she was the only woman to hold such a position in Britain.

Nimmo's red star logo was first switched on as a neon sign at one of their houses in 1951. The company went public in 1952 and in 1957 the company claimed to have opened the most modern malting plant in the north of England. In 1958, the company expanded into the foreign territory that was Tyneside with the acquisition of Davison & Wood of Gateshead, including their twenty public houses.

Whitbread acquired J Nimmo & Son in September 1963, along with 125 public houses, for £2.25 million. Whitbread announced that it would retain the Nimmo name and expand production which it developed to an annual capacity of 220,000 barrels that included the renowned Mackeson Stout following the closure of the Exchange Brewery in Sheffield. In 1998 the brewery went into private ownership and the brewing of Castle Eden Ales continued apace.

The brewery was closed down in 2002, and production was moved down the coast to Cameron's Brewery in Hartlepool. Cameron's announced the return of Castle Eden Ale production in 2013. In 2014, the brewery assets were acquired by the present owners and relocated to Seaham. Since 2016, the brewery has focused on providing contract brewing and packaging whilst continuing to offer a range of Castle Eden Ales on draught.

Reflecting the importance of mining to the local economy in 1892 Nimmo's had five pubs called the Colliery Inn (at Castle Eden, Shotton, Sacriston, Trimdon and Ludworth) and one named the Davy Lamp Inn at Easington Lane near Hetton-le-Hole. Nimmo's pubs in Newcastle were: Stag's Head, Gibson Street, (closed 1965) and Dun Cow, Back Eldon Street, (closed 1962). To the south there were pubs in West Hartlepool: Royal Hotel, Alma Hotel, Central Hotel, and the Royal Hotel in Redcar. There were eight houses in Seaham Harbour and two in Sunderland.

North Eastern Breweries,
Sunderland

North Eastern Breweries Ltd, Wear Brewery, Westbourne Road, Sunderland was registered December 1896 with over 250 houses formed from Bramwell & Co, Wear Brewery; William Story & Co, Moor Street Brewery, Sunderland; Richard Murray, wine, spirit and ale merchants and aerated water manufacturer, Consett; J H Graham, Middlesborough, wine and spirit merchant; Patrick Bruce Junor, Tower Brewery, Tudhoe Grange, Spennymoor and Thomas Elwen, Frederick Street, Sunderland, ale and porter merchants.

Newcastle pubs included: Volunteer Arms, Sunderland Street; Graham Arms, Scotswood Road; Royal Sovereign, Cut Bank; Hope & Anchor, Horatio Street; Barrack Tavern, Barrack Road; Jingling Gate Inn, Throckley; Ridley Inn, Pilgrim Street; Tiger Inn, Bedford Street, North Shields; Blandford Inn, Blandford Street. There were also fifty pubs in and around Middlesbrough and North Yorkshire, including four in Redcar, Marske and Saltburn.

In 1912 North East Breweries still owned twenty-six Sunderland pubs, roughly the same as Newcastle Breweries, despite the enormous number of pub closures. More than half the Newcastle Breweries were in Monkwearmouth.

W B Reid & Co. Ltd.

Leazes Brewery, Upper Claremont, The Leazes,
Newcastle-upon-Tyne.

Founded 1837 and registered May 1891 to acquire W B Reid & Co, Leazes Brewery; Reid Brothers & Co, wine and spirit merchants, Newcastle and the licensed houses belonging to the Tyne Brewery Co. Ltd. W.B. Reid bought the eight houses owned by James Chrisp, including the Ship Isis. As noted, W.B. Reid & Co was another new enterprise born of mergers in 1891 who went on to become the second biggest public house owners in 1892 with thirty houses and owning 154 in their entire sales area by the time of their takeover by William Younger in 1956 with 154 tied houses.

John Rowell & Sons Ltd.,
Gateshead

Their New Brewery was established on Gateshead High Street in 1840. Rowell was expansionist, taking over the businesses of J.M Bruce, Wm Turnbull & Co of Ferry Brewery South Shields, Gilpin & Co mineral water manufacturers, Newcastle, and Matthew Taylor & Co of Swalwell. The Gateshead Brewery Co came along in 1912. An attempt on Tucker's was unsuccessful and they were themselves taken over by Newcastle Breweries.

Their pubs included Grace Darling, Scotswood, Newcastle; Lord Clyde Inn, Byker, Newcastle; Plumber's Arms, Newcastle (closed 1935); Colliery Hotel, Pelton Fell, near Chester le Street; Grey Horse Inn, Pelton; Dun Cow, Shildon; Bee Hive Inn, Shotton Colliery Gateshead pubs included Barley Mow, East Street; Black Swan, Park Lane; Blue Bell, High Street; Cricketer's Arms, Prince Consort Road; Honeysuckle Hotel, Coatsworth Road; and the Vulcan Inn, Quarryfield Road.

Barge Inn in Hillgate

http://www.gateshead-history.com/gateshead-pubs.html

The sire contains a marvellous listing of old Gateshead pubs by street with some wonderful images. A John Bratton website

Sandyford Brewery,
Newcastle

This is named Sandyford Stone Brewery on the 2nd edition OS mapping. A brewery was in existence here in the eighteenth century, ran by a Mr Joseph Naiters. The family lived at Sandyford House. By the end of the century his sons, Nicholas and Ralph took over. Ralph was also in partnership with Henry Weatherley, with wine and spirit cellars on The Side. In 1812 quantities of worked stone chippings were found beneath the banks of the stream near Lambert's Leap. This may have been the site of the quarry for the original brewery, hence the name Sandyford Stone. Nicholas Naiters died in 1822 and Ralph Naiters carried on the business until his death in 1863. In 1863 the business passed to J.S. Arnison, Naiters' son-in-law. From the late 1880s Robert Deuchar leased it and bought it on Arnison's death in 1892. The brewery bonded warehouse … is listed grade 2. Pediment has 'OFFICE 1904 Robert Deuchar Ltd' in panels. The brewery boiler house is also listed grade 2. Both buildings date to circa 1840.'[Source: https://sitelines.newcastle.gov.uk/SMR/4141]

Scottish & Newcastle Ltd,
Newcastle

It all started with Grizel Syme who ran her late second husband's brewery: this brewery and those of her sons developed into William Younger & Co. Ltd, Abbey & Holyrood Breweries, Edinburgh merging with William McEwan & Co. Ltd, Fountain Brewery, Fountainbridge, Edinburgh in 1931 to form Scottish Brewers. Thomas & James Bernard Ltd of Edinburgh were acquired in April 1960 and their brewery closed. In 1960, they merged with Newcastle Breweries Ltd to form Scottish & Newcastle Breweries Ltd.

By 1985, the company had become a regional brewer focused on Scotland and the north of England, ranked number five in the UK and selling around 6 Mhl per annum. A decade later, with the purchase of rival Courage, S&N had become the UK's leading brewer, producing around 15 Mhl per annum. Its UK brewing division became known as Scottish Courage but this reverted to S&N UK in February 2006. In 2004 some savage cost-cutting measures were introduced to reduce an inflated cost base. That year, the Fountain Brewery in Edinburgh was closed, followed by the Tyne Brewery in Newcastle. Reciprocal acquisitions saw the Caledonian Brewery in Edinburgh and the Northern Clubs' Federation Brewery in Gateshead added to the business.

On 31 March 2008, shareholders approved the £7.8 billion takeover by Heineken and Carlsberg. On 23 November 2009, the company changed its name to Heineken UK Ltd. to reflect the owner's name. Scottish & Newcastle employed 40,000 people in the United Kingdom and mainland Europe; their breweries included: The Fountain Brewery, Edinburgh - closed 2004; The Tyne Brewery, Newcastle-upon-Tyne - closed 2005; The Federation Brewery, Gateshead - bought 2004, closed 2010; T & R Theakston's Brewery, Masham (S&N had a majority holding in this brewery. It is now once again owned by the Theakston family); John Smith's Brewery, Tadcaster.

Newcastle Brown Ale and James Porter

Everything and everyone is iconic nowadays, even the most mediocre of people and the most middling and commonplace of things. However, there remains some things which can be called iconic with justification because they do rise above the average. One of those things is Newcastle Brown Ale; even if you don't care for it particularly, or for beer generally, you have to admit that its branding and the symbolism it projects is exceptional. It champions northern beers, the city of Newcastle and, for many, not all, north eastern life generally, just as the Beatles and Liverpool FC do Liverpool, and Oasis and Manchester United Manchester.

Newcastle Brown Ale is a brown ale, launched in 1927 by Colonel Jim Porter after three years of painstaking development and endless tasting. The 1960 merger of Newcastle Breweries with Scottish Brewers bestowed upon the beer the national distribution and sales it needed by the early 1970s. A welcome resurgence in the late 1980s and early 1990s went down a treat boosted by a thirsty market in savvy student unions. By the late 1990s, Newcastle Brown was the most widely distributed alcoholic product in the UK. Even though the 2000s saw the majority of sales in the United States (there are lots more people there after all), it still sells 100 million bottles annually in the UK. Brewing moved in 2005 from Newcastle to Dunston, Tyne and Wear, in 2010 to Tadcaster, and in 2017 to the Heineken Brewery in Zoeterwoude, the Netherlands. As of 2019, it is also brewed by Lagunitas Brewing Company in Petaluma, California, and Chicago, for the American market.

Just like Cameron's Strongarm down the coast in Hartlepool, Newcastle Brown Ale is of course perceived in the UK as a working-man's and woman's beer, with an adamantine association with heavy industry, once the traditional economic bedrock of the north east of England. It was one of the first beers to be sold in a clear glass bottle.

James Herbert Porter was born in Burton upon Trent in 1892 and became a third-generation brewer at Newcastle Breweries in 1909. World War I intervened, and Porter served in the North Staffordshire Regiment earning his DSO with Bar for gallantry.

After the war, Porter returned to Newcastle Breweries and was charged with satisfying the rising demand for a bottled beer with a kick in the early 1920s. As assistant brewer, Porter worked alongside the firm's chief chemist, Archie Jones, to refine a new formula: after endless modifications and tastings this was to become Newcastle Brown Ale. When Porter completed the beer, he was not happy with it, as he had actually been attempting to recreate Bass ale. Nevertheless it was to be an enormous success. The original beer had an original gravity of 1060° and was 6.25 ABV; it sold at a premium price of 9 shillings for a dozen pint bottles. Newcastle Brown Ale started to come off the production line at Tyne Brewery in 1927 and when first marketed in 1927 it won all seven major awards at the 1928 Breweries Exhibition.

The blue star logo was introduced to the Newcastle Brown Ale bottle in 1928, the instantly recognisable five points of the star representing the five founding breweries of Newcastle Breweries.

After the merger of Scottish Brewers with Newcastle Breweries in 1960, Newcastle Brown Ale became a flagship brand of Scottish & Newcastle alongside McEwan's Export and Younger's Tartan Special.

The fame of Newcastle Brown's growing worldwide popularity spurred an Australian brewer to launch a hostile bid for the company in 1988. This attempted seizure, fostered an intense backlash in Newcastle, with locals passionately rallying behind our "Keep Us on Top!" campaign. As a sign of solidarity, the Newcastle Brown label was inverted until the takeover was quashed.

In 1997, Scottish and Newcastle claimed that it was the most widely distributed alcoholic product in both pubs and off licences in the country.

Porter became managing director of Newcastle Breweries in 1931; five years later, he was appointed to the Institute of Brewing's Council, and he served as its president between 1939 and 1941. In 1953 Porter was vice-chairman of Newcastle Breweries and two years later became its chairman. Following the company's merger with Scottish Breweries in 1960, he became the group's vice-chairman and subsequently its vice-president. He died on 22 March 1973, aged 81, leaving a widow, two daughters and one son, Henry, who became chairman of Newcastle Breweries and a director at Newcastle and Scottish Breweries.

In the North East, Newcastle Brown Ale is often given the nickname "Dog", alluding to the British euphemism of seeing a man about a dog. It is also known as Broon, "brown" pronounced in the Geordie dialect. Elsewhere in the UK, it is known as 'Newkie Brown'.

https://www.brandme.co.uk/case-studies/newcastle-brown-ale

Isaac Tucker & Co. Ltd.,
Gateshead

Their Turk's Head Brewery, 13 West Street, Gateshead, opened in 1790 and was reputed in 1891 to be "the first to introduce pale ale into the neighbourhood"; Isaac Tucker joined the firm somewhat later. His son's (Thomas') obituary in 1891 speaks of 100 employees and forty horses. Tuckers swallowed up James Robinson & Son Ltd in 1932 but fell to Whitbread in 1932 when they had 30 on the payroll and 50 tied houses.

Tucker delivery, and their interesting Dinner Ale

Vaux,
Sunderland

'Vaux has been a beloved name in Sunderland for almost 200 years. From the earliest incarnation of 'C. Vaux & Sons' in 1837 right through to the 1990s, the brewery was an important part of city life in Sunderland until its closure in 1999'.

So proclaims the www.vaux.beer website having re-launched this iconic iconic brand in 2019 when they opened their Monk Street brewery and taproom in 2021.

Early Vaux branding

This famous company was founded around 1805 by Cuthbert Vaux (1779–1850) in partnership with a Mr W Story at Moor Street Brewery. In 1850 son Cuthbert took over the business until his death in 1878 when sons John Storey Vaux (d. 1881) and Colonel Edwin Vaux took control as partners. In 1896 the company was registered as C. Vaux & Sons Ltd at a brewery on the corner of Matlock and Cumberland Street west of the present Wearmouth Bridge. Expansion necessitated moves, first to Union Street then to Castle Street in 1875. Cuthbert served his apprenticeship with Carlsberg in Copenhagen, and returned home to make Vaux one of the first brewers to move into bottling ales and stouts.

His son Ernest, through his military experience with a Maxim gun, gave the name to Vaux's most famous beer. And then there was sister Amy who, in 1898, married chartered accountant Frank Nicholson. He brought management skills to her brothers' brewing expertise, and hauled the business out of the Victorian age and into the 20th century.

Vaux always were disadvantaged by a lack of owned or tied houses in Sunderland, their strength lying in the Durham mining towns and in Middlesbrough. In 1892 Sunderland firm William St John & Annison (who in 1895 themselves bought Penny Hill Brewery, Holbeach, Lincolnshire) could claim a larger Sunderland estate with thirty-one houses, while Newcastle Breweries had twenty eight with Vaux and James Deuchar at twenty-two each of the 417 houses in the borough. William Jackson had fifteen houses. This at a time when at least ten breweries vied for market share. Brewers owned about 100 of these houses. Landowner Sir William Hedworth it was who sold out to Deuchars while Newcastle's W.B. Reid bought the eight houses owned by James Chrisp, including the Ship Isis. Meanwhile brewers Bramwell & Co was swallowed up by Spennymoor-based North Eastern Brewers and T.E. Chapman by West Hartlepool's J.W. Cameron in 1897. Alloa brewer George Younger bought R. Fenwick & Co the following year. In 1906 the influx continued with the arrival in Sunderland of George Mackay & Co of Edinburgh and the Tadcaster Tower Brewery Co.

Ernest was a redoubtable soldier, mentioned seven times in despatches during the Boer War in which he served with the Northumberland Hussars. The Maxim gun was named after its inventor, Sir Hiram Stevens Maxim, who also invented a steam-driven bi-plane and patented an early hair curling iron before going deaf due to over-exposure to the noise of his machine gun.

Sadly, having served in the Boer War and World War I, in 1925, during a dinner party at home at Brettonby, Lt-Col Vaux – choked on a rabbit bone and died.

The Northern Echo (16th March 2019) tells us how 'Using the railway network, Vaux expanded. Bottling plants were set up from Leeds to Glasgow, including Spennymoor and Middlesbrough, and hogsheads of Sunderland-brewed beer were despatched by train to be bottled at the plants and then distributed locally by horse-drawn drays'.

In 1923 Vaux swallowed up J. Heslop, brewers in Stockton-on-Tees and in 1925, with James Calder & Co they bought out Robinson Brothers of Houghton le Spring. But the game changer was the takeover of North Eastern Breweries.

The Northern Echo tell us how 'the biggest decision came in 1927 when Vaux took over North Eastern Breweries (NEB). NEB was a much bigger company – created by the amalgamation of small local breweries, including Tower of Spennymoor, Harkers of Hartlepool and Warwicks of Rise Carr in Darlington – but, in the depths of the depression, it was in dire economic straits'. The Vaux-NEB company became Associated Breweries Ltd in 1927.

A busy yard at Vaux

Expansion contined unabated into the 1930s, through the 1940s, and into the early 1950s, with the acquisition of a further five breweries including Lorimer & Clark Ltd, their first Scottish brewery. The name was Vaux & Associated breweries from 1940. During the 1950s a further three Scottish breweries were added including Thomas Usher & Son Ltd and Steel, Coulson & Co. Ltd, both based in Edinburgh in 1959 and John Wright & Co. (Perth) Ltd in 1961.

The name changed to Vaux Breweries Ltd in 1973. By 1975 they held 789 houses in England and 200 Thomas Usher & Son Ltd houses in Scotland. In the early days the company developed popular brands including Highly Nourishing Stout, India Pale Ale, Vaux's Stout, Maxim, Double Maxim, and Sunderland Best Bitter.

Vaux pubs trespassing into Newcastle include: the Kenton Bar Inn, Percy Arms, Tanners Arms, Windmill Inn, Rose & Crown and the Half Moon Hotel in Byker.

Times were changing rapidly and, under Margaret Thatcher, the north-east was de-industrialising: the 'government wanted to promote competition within the brewing industry so it strove to break the link between the big brewers and their tied pubs – between Vaux and its 888 outlets'.

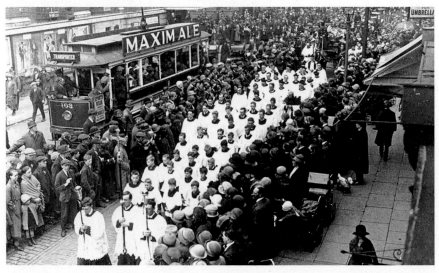

Maxim promotion, probably at Easter

Here is the long history of Vaux takeovers:

1923	John Heslop Ltd's Norton Grange Brewery, Norton-on-Tees, was acquired
1925	Robinson Brothers of Houghton-le-Spring was partially acquired
1927	Merged with North Eastern Breweries Ltd to form Associated Breweries Ltd.
1937	They acquired Berwick Breweries Ltd and closed the breweries.
1938	They acquired Ridley, Cutter & Firth Ltd of Newcastle-upon-Tyne, and brewing ceased.
1927	Merged with North Eastern Breweries Ltd to form Associated Breweries Ltd.
1937	They acquired Berwick Breweries Ltd and closed the breweries.
1938	They acquired Ridley, Cutter & Firth Ltd of Newcastle-upon-Tyne, and brewing ceased.
1943	They acquired Coldstream Brewery Co. Ltd in November.
1946	They acquired Lorimer & Clark Ltd of Edinburgh. This brewery was sold to its management in May 1987, and continues to brew as Caledonian Brewery Co. Ltd.
1947	They acquired Whitwell, Mark & Co. Ltd of Kendal with 30 tied houses. Brewing ceased there on 18th September 1968.
1947	Hepworth & Co. Ltd of Ripon were acquired with about 51 pubs and brewing ceased there in 1952.
1959	Thomas Usher & Son Ltd of Edinburgh were acquired with 170 public houses. Sold to Allied Breweries in 1980.
1959	They acquired Steel, Coulson & Co. Ltd of Edinburgh and Glasgow.
1961	They acquired John Wright & Co (Perth) Ltd.
1970s	They acquired Liefman's Brewery, Oudenaarde, Belgium, but sold it off in 1985.
1972	They acquired Ward & Co. Ltd of Sheffield with 102 tied houses which had been making beer in Sheffield since 1830, and closed that brewery in 1999.
1978	W M Darley Ltd of Thorne, Yorkshire, were acquired with 88 houses. Darley's Brewery was closed in September 1986.

[Source: breweryhistory.com/wiki/index.php?title=Vaux_Breweries_Ltd]

In addition the group supplied over 1,000 clubs and about 4,000 free houses.

By the early 1990s the Vaux Group had expanded into hotels but March 1999 saw their parent company, the Swallow Group (formerly the Vaux Group), decide to axe the breweries in Sunderland and Sheffield after 162 years of brewing to concentrate on its hotel and restaurant chains. The following year the company was taken over by Whitbread and most of the hotels became Marriotts; the larger pubs were brought under other national brands - such as Brewers Fayre.

In 2000, two former Vaux directors and the former head brewer formed what is now called the Maxim Brewery based in Houghton-le-Spring, buying some of the beer brands and recipes. They resurrected the famous Samson and Double Maxim brown ale lines under the name the Double Maxim Beer Company. In 2003, the company bought the brand and recipes of a former Vaux subsidiary, Wards, and re-launched Wards Best Bitter. The renamed Maxim Brewery is now the biggest independent brewery in the north east.

The impressive mural in the tap room.

Maxim was first brewed in 1901 to celebrate the return of the Maxim Gun detachment from the Boer War which was commanded by Colonel Ernest Vaux; this brown ale is one of the oldest surviving beers in the United Kingdom. In 1938, the strength of the original Maxim beer was increased to 4.7 per cent, and it was renamed Double Maxim so that it could give Newcastle Brown a run for its money. The brew still carries with it the promise of "Full of Northern Character". The man who made the beer in Sunderland, Jim Murray, now oversees its production in Stockport by Robinson's brewery.

OTHER BREWERIES

Archibald Arrol & Sons Ltd, came from Alloa (where else?); they were founded in 1810 by Andrew Roy and owned a number of Tyneside houses. Registered May 1895 to amalgamate Walter and Archibald Arrol with John Meikle (Arthur's Hill Brewery) and acquire some houses from William Turnbull & Co, both of Newcastle-upon-Tyne. Acquired by **Allsopp & Sons Ltd** of Burton-upon-Trent in 1930 who had some with some Gateshead pubs to their name including the Alma, British Lion and Victoria. Later traded as Ind Coope Alloa Brewery Ltd and then as the Alloa Brewery Co. Ltd. Closed 1998.

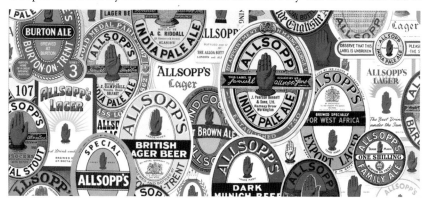

Changing marketing methods over the years.

H. Fail & Co of Gateshead worked closely with the firm of John Rowell & Sons. Henry Fail managed the Honeysuckle Hotel; other houses included the Globe, the Neville and the Barley Mow.

Davison and Wood of West Street Gateshead got together in 1893; the company was bought by Nimmo in 1959. Before that their flagship pub was the Half Moon Hotel. Other locals included the Peareth Arms, Rector House, the Talbot and the Brown Jug Arms.

Swinburne & Co were originally brewers but moved over to wine and spirit merchants in 1890 with eleven tied houses. They managed some of the higher end establishments, including the Royal Hotel, the Queen's Hotel and the Central. Part of the Newcastle Brewery consortium.

Robinson and Anderson. We have already met 'Tot' who was publican at the William IV on Bottle Bank; in the 1930s the family moved over the road to the Old Nag's Head. The firm assumed the tenancy of the **James Calder & Co** pubs and owned the Plough on East Street among others. The James Calder Shore Brewery, Alloa was built in 1816. Records held at the University of Glasgow Archives tell us that:

Swinburne's Dun Cow

'The company was re-registered as James Calder & Co (Brewers) Ltd in 1920 and its whisky interests were sold to James Dewar & Sons. Brewing ceased at the Shore Brewery in 1921, all the company's brewing requirements being contracted out to Archibald Arrol & Sons Ltd [until 1951 when John Jeffrey & Co. Ltd. brewed for them after the conversion of the Alloa Brewery into a lager only plant]. The company acquired a brewery at Ostend, Belgium, for £12,718 in 1921 and, with C Vaux & Sons Ltd, Sunderland, England, also took over Robinson Brothers Ltd, Houghton-le-Spring, Sunderland with 63 tied houses in 1925, dividing the houses between themselves. It also acquired Arrol's Scottish tied houses in the late 1930s; breweries in Marsa, Malta, and Nairobi, Kenya; Robert Henderson & Co Ltd, The Mills Brewery, Alloa, Scotland, in 1944; Steel Coulson & Co Ltd 's Greenhead Brewery, Glasgow, in 1946; and Geo Thomson & Son Ltd, bottlers of Falkirk; Blairgowrie, Perthshire and Kinross; and Dysart, Fife, in 1950.

- archiveshub.jisc.ac.uk/search/archives/a3729d22-35ed-3884-9543-f36407a81921

If nothing else the James Calder backstory demonstrated the fluidity of the industry when it comes to mergers and takeovers, the possible diversity of product, the cooperation between companies and the international opportunities – rare but possible, nevertheless. One of their better known pubs was the Crawshay Inn.

See also www.breweryhistory.com/Defunct/BreweryIndex.htm

MICROBREWERIES
a selection

Wylam Brewery, Newcastle

Wylam Brewery at Exhibition Park's Palace of Arts is a 30 barrel microbrewery. As well as the Brewery there is a Brewery Tap and Kitchen, which is open Thursdays to Sundays each week 'and serves the best in craft beer both on keg and cask including their famous Jakehead IPA, range of Heritage Cask Beers and core keg beers'.

Founded in 2000 in a potting shed in the village of Wylam in Northumberland, today Wylam Brewery is the last remaining building from the 1929 North East Exhibition. The Exhibition was an ambitious project built to celebrate and encourage Craft, Art and Industry at the start of the Great Depression. Being in the Grade 2 listed Palace of Arts, Wylam can comfortably lay claim to the title of the UK's most picturesque brewery.

A fully operational in-house microbrewery has been installed in the **Bridge Tavern** in association with Wylam Brewery.

Wylam Brewery at Palace of Arts, Claremont Road, Newcastle upon Tyne, NE2 4PZ

Anarchy Brew Co. first took to the streets in 2012 in Morpeth. October 2018 saw the brewery move to a bigger site in Walkergate, Newcastle upon Tyne, with the addition of a new taproom playing host to tap takeovers, brewer meet-ups, gigs, DJ sets etc. Beers from Anarchy Brew Co. can now be found across the globe, proving popular in Russia (well, maybe not now), Italy, Finland, and many other countries, and with recent collaborations with 7 Fjell Bryggeri (Norway); the brewery continues to go from strength to strength.

> *Telephone: 0191 389 7580 • Website: www.anarchybrewco.com*

Box Social Brewing – a 15 UK Barrel Micro-Brewery based in Newburn, Newcastle-Upon-Tyne complete with tasting room. Where did that name come from? The website tells us that 'In Victorian Britain, middle-class people had few acceptable ways to socialise and meet new people. A solution emerged, that solution was "box socials", events held at various people's houses where they could mix in a risk-free environment. We are taking "Box Socials" into the 21st century, connecting people over great artisan craft beer'. *[www.boxsocial.pub]*

Tyne Bank Brewery and Tap Room

The website tells how 'Inspired by the brewing scene on the West Coast of America Julia Austin founded Tyne Bank Brewery in 2011. Building on the north's historic love of beer, our craft ales soon became so popular we outgrew our first home. So, in 2016 we invested and crowdfunded, to relocate to our new home, an industrial-style, 13,000 sq ft warehouse with tap room and events space on the edge of Ouseburn, home to Newcastle's vibrant creative community just a short stroll from the city centre. Here drinkers can enjoy a pint whilst watching the brewhouse in action'. There are brewery tours which include an introduction to the brewing process, a brief history of the Brewery and the opportunity for a tutored tasting. *[www.tynebankbrewery. co.uk/the-brewery]*

Hadrian Border Brewery

Following the takeover of the Border Brewery in Berwick which dates back to 1777 and later The Four Rivers Brewery (formerly Hadrian Brewery) in Byker, the brewery now operates out of a 40 barrel plant in Newburn.

Unit 5, The Preserving Works, Newburn Industrial Estate, Shelley Rd, Newcastle upon Tyne NE15 9RT • Telephone: 0191 264 9000
E-mail: info@hadrian-border-brewery.co.uk
Website: www.hadrian-border-brewery.co.uk

The Keelman and Big Lamp Brewery, Newburn

A pub and microbrewery Pub and Micro Brewery on the Hadrian's Wall cross country walk. he Big Lamp Brewery has been going since 1982 and is the oldest microbrewery in the North East. See entry above.

Northern Alchemy (Crafty Beer)

After three years of operating in The Lab (a shipping container next to the Cumberland Arms), and cuckoo brewing, Northern Alchemy moved to their current home, converting a former coal depot into a new and vibrant brewery, named The Old Coal Yard.

***The Old Coal Yard,** Elizabeth Street, Newcastle upon Tyne NE6 1JS*
Email: info@northernalchemy.co.uk • Website: www.northernalchemy.co.uk

TEMPERANCE

In a book that is fulsome in its praise for the British pub, it is only right to complete the story by remembering that not everyone in the nation has always been enamoured by pubs, inns, taverns and alehouses or by the imbibing of alcohol. Indeed, some people eschew such establishments completely and, for various good reasons, avoid beer and other alcoholic beverages. To provide a degree of context and balance it is important to look at temperance and abstinence, especially as it has related to the north-east.

The earliest temperance societies were inspired by Belfast professor of theology, and Presbyterian Church of Ireland minister John Edgar, who famously and conclusively poured his stash of whisky out of the window in 1829. Joseph Livesey underwrote his philanthropic work in temperance with the profits he made from cheese production. The word teetotal comes from a speech by Richard (Dickie) Turner, a follower of Livesey, in Preston in 1833, with not a little help from his stutter: "I'll be reet down out-and-out t-t-total for ever and ever". Others, however, contend that the name "teetotaler" came from the capital "T"s that were written next to the names of people who pledged complete abstinence from alcohol.

Livesey opened the first temperance hotel in 1833 and the next year founded the first temperance magazine, *The Preston Temperance Advocate* (1834–37). The British Association for the Promotion of Temperance was established by 1835 and had as its mission statement 'Education for all'. A contemporary pamphlet urges residents to *'come as you are, do not stoop to black your boots'*.

In 1847, the Band of Hope Union was founded in Leeds, the aim of which was saving working class children from the perils of drink. The members were obliged to pledge to abstain "from all liquors of an intoxicating quality, whether ale, porter, wine or ardent spirits, except as medicine". Their *Hymn Book*, published in 1881, sold nearly three million copies. The Cadets of Temperance was another organisation, targeting children to preach the perils of drink. In Newcastle the

Union in 1894 went so far as to build the fountain near the junction of Cloth and Groat Markets; its inscription bears the cautionary words of wisdom 'water is best'. How many of the patrons of the sixteen pubs flourishing in the market area would have subscribed to that? Cloth Market had eight – one for every three buildings – which included the Wheatsheaf (Balmbra's), the Old Durham House (later Presidents), the Imperial Hotel (Bewicks), the Old George and the Bee Hive – the latter two still pulling pints.

The Heaton Anti-Licensing Council was particularly careful when granting licences for new public houses; in fact it would be more accurate to say that they ardently opposed the granting of licences. Only two pubs were built in Heaton in the late 19th and early 20th centuries: the Chillingham Hotel and the Corner House leading to the densely populated suburb being described as a 'dry area'.

General Neal Dow in Maine, United States in 1851 introduced the Maine Law prohibiting the sale of intoxicants. In 1853, this inspired the formation of the United Kingdom Alliance in Manchester; it was made up of a hard-line group of prohibitionists to advocate, divisively, a similar law prohibiting the sale of alcohol in the UK. The idea was initiated by Nathaniel Card (1805–1856), an Irish cotton manufacturer and member of the Society of Friends (Quakers). He had earlier been a member of the Manchester and Salford Temperance Society. Members believed that temperance societies fail until legal temptations for drink and drunkenness were abolished. They aimed for legislative suppression of traffic in intoxicating beverages. On 14 February 1853, the name of the organisation changed to the United Kingdom Alliance for the Suppression of the Traffic in all Intoxicating Liquors to reflect this.

The Alliance was opposed by less radical temperance organisations who preferred moral persuasion to a legal ban. The impotence of legislation in this field became all too clear when the Sale of Beer Act 1854 which restricted Sunday opening hours had to be repealed, following widespread rioting. In 1859 a prototype prohibition bill was overwhelmingly defeated in the House of Commons.

In 1862 the Church of England Total Abstinence Society was founded, 'which rested on a broader basis than the Alliance, and more truly represented the British flair for compromise'.

The US-based (but international) Woman's Christian Temperance Union (WCTU) was founded in 1873, becoming one of the world's largest women's societies in the 19th century, campaigning for temperance and women's suffrage. In 1876 the British Women's Temperance Association was formed by women to persuade men to stop drinking, rebranded in 2006 as the White Ribbon Association.

One of the most active advocates of temperance was Dr. Norman Shanks Kerr. He promoted the treatment of inebriates and held that inebriety was a disease, not a vice, and that it should be treated accordingly. In 1884, in response to the inadequacy of the Habitual Drunkards Act of 1879, he founded the Society for the Study and Cure of Inebriety and was the first president. It exists today as the Society for the Study of Addiction.

In 1884 the National Temperance Federation, which was associated with the Liberal Party, was founded as an umbrella organisation. The Conservative Party largely supported the interests of the alcohol industry and opposed temperance.

In 1882 the United Kingdom Alliance produced a map showing all the licensed premises in Newcastle-upon-Tyne: this comprised the 446 licensed houses (pubs), 324 beer houses, 36 breweries and 77 off licenses – a total of 883 places where alcohol could be purchased. The map shows a concentration in the small area around the Town Hall and the Bigg, Cloth and Grote markets where 23 pubs and four beer houses plied their trade. The number of establishments had been growing since 1778 when there was 11 pubs and 17 in 1837 –figures which are consistent with the population growth in Newcastle generally and the mid-Victorian rise in beer consumption. In the late 1870s beer production in Britain exceeded 30 million barrels per year; weekly consumption averaged over five pints for every man, woman and child. Growth in the brewing industry was consonant with this rising demand with smaller breweries yielding to larger ones with their wider reach. Interestingly, despite the increase in real wages and disposable income individual beer consumption remained much the same as people found other ways to enjoy their leisure time, for example on day trips facilitated by the railways. Competition amongst breweries sharpened as they vied with each other to secure accounts with any and every pub – a feverish climate which encouraged breweries to build better and grander pubs in which the drinking experience got better and better – in short a showplace for each brewer's beer offer. The pubs around Bigg Market, for example, were contenders in this scramble for market share.

TEMP1

Nathaniel Currier (1813–1888) and **James Merritt Ives (1824–1895)** produced over thirty prints that focussed graphically on the Temperance Movement. This one shows a semi-circle of male figures beginning with Step 1. "A glass with a Friend" up and over semi-circle to Step 9 "Death by suicide." Half circle bottom center with an image of a weeping woman walking with a child.

Steps:

1. A glass with a Friend
2. A glass to keep the cold out
3. A glass too much
4. Drunk and riotous
5. The Summit attained; Jolly Companions; a confirmed Drunkard
6. Poverty and Disease
7. Forsaken by Friends
8. Desperation and crime
9. Death by suicide

THE DRUNKARDS PROGRESS
FROM THE FIRST GLASS TO THE GRAVE.

TEMP2

William Meacham Murrell's equally evocative 1846 Map of Temperance. The website tells us that it is 'An early allegorical map on temperance, accompanied by a lengthy poem. Typical of "didactic" visual aids intended to be "at once entertaining and instructive... colorful and intricate temperance maps depicting the 'Ocean of Life' trained viewers to see that the path to damnation was... a veritable riptide towing the sinner from the first sip of grog to the channel of destruction. The apparent innocuousness and swift danger of water made it a potent metaphor for life's temptations in an era when waterways were primary transportation routes, and accidental drownings and shipwrecks not uncommon. The maps vividly showed that 'Religion Channel' was just one strong current away from 'Misery Regions' and the 'Reprobate Empire,' not only for seasoned tipplers but for all on the 'Ocean of Life.'"

www.digital.library.cornell.edu/catalog/ss:3293739

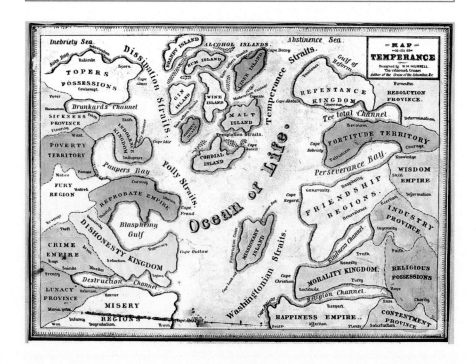

Kelley's Directory 1929

Lists the following Temperance hotels in Newcastle:
- **Cassidy**, run by Miss Francis, 104 Newgate Street
- **Clyde**, Miss N. Cleverly, 18 Westmoreland Road
- **Empire Temperance Hotel**, 1 Nun's Lane
- **Hume,** Miss Jane, 18 Wentworth Place
- **Livingstone, J.** , 52 Newgate Street
- **Portland Commercial**, 21 Portland terrace
- **Punton, Mrs E.,** 14 Bath lane
- **Queen's Hotel,** 37 Westmoreland Road
- **Tyne Temperance Hotel**, 13 Hood Street, Whinship's Hotel, 75 Clayton Street

Secular temperance organisations connected to the labour movement started to emerge, for example the Scottish Prohibition Party, founded by a communist temperance activist called Bob Stewart; a Marxist offshoot called the Prohibition and Reform Party, which later became part of the Communist Party of Great Britain in 1920.

The former Manchester City FC football stadium, Maine Road, gets its name from a renaming of Dog Kennel Lane by members of the Temperance Movement, inspired by the 1853 Maine law.

There was also the Clarendon in Clayton Street. There were others in Alnwick, Berwick, Morpeth, Wallsend and Whitley Bay. Four of Kelley's hotels were run by women.

Religion played a part: various Nonconformist groups - the Methodists, Quakers and The Salvation Army (founded 1864), lobbied parliament to restrict alcohol sales. In Wales, Lady Llanover, motivated by Calvinistic Methodists teachings, closed all the public houses on her estate and was an outspoken critic of the evil drink. The Church of England Temperance Society was founded in 1862; its volunteers in the court system led to the first probation service. The League of the Cross was a Catholic total abstinence organisation founded in 1873 by Cardinal Manning. As noted above in 1876 the British Women's Temperance Association was formed to persuade men to stop drinking, rebranded in 2006 as the White Ribbon Association.

The battle for temperance, then, was hard fought; it may be that those who fought the fight believed that if only one drinker was dissuaded from the drink then the arduous fight was well worth it. In the event, it is estimated that in 1900 10% of the adult population was teetotal. That must be considered a success. At the same time, we know that beer drinking was on the decline with 138 pubs calling time for the last time.

The pub was not helped by the First World War during which it was standard practice for (mainly male) workers in restricted occupations to have a drink before work and in the lunch break. This had a detrimental effect on productivity, particularly in munitions; so bad was it that David Lloyd George said in February 1915 when querying the reasons behind the shortfall in output: 'let us be perfectly candid. It is mostly the lure of the drink...drink is doing more damage in the war than all the German submarines put together'. Duty on alcoholic beverages was raised, shorter opening hours were imposed, and alcoholic drinks were watered down. These measures had the desired effect: pubs closed in their droves. In 1931 a Royal Commission was able to declare that getting drunk had gone out of fashion; in modern parlance, it was no longer cool.

So, in passing the Defence of the Realm Act in 1914 the Liberal Government gave temperance an unexpected boost: pub hours were reduced, beer was subject to a penny a pint extra tax; the momentum was maintained by the subsequent State Management Scheme in 1916 which nationalised breweries and pubs in certain areas of Britain where armaments manufacture was taking place.

In 1931 the True Temperance Movement complained that Carlisle where, unlike the rest of the country, its pubs remained in state ownership, cases of drunkenness were running at 9.58 per 10,000 population while in Liverpool it was 4.2 and 4.1 in Newcastle, 2.4 in Birmingham and Salford, 1.3 in Leeds and a comparatively sober 0.8 in Bristol. What does that say about Nationalisation?

Vimto, originally "Vim Tonic", was concocted in 1908 as a healthy alternative to alcohol, and originally sold in temperance bars. Fitzpatrick's Herbal Health in Rawtenstall, Lancashire, is thought to be the oldest surviving temperance bar.

Coffee Houses

A degree of civilisation and sobriety had arrived with the emergence of the coffee house. Coffee-houses of all complexions – salubrious and salacious alike - were all the rage in the 17th and 18th centuries. Coffee houses embodied temperance to some degree and were not just about coffee drinking. The more civilised establishments were not only convivial, sober and convenient places to meet for artists, politicians, dandies about town and writers; serious business and banking transactions took place in them; Freemasons had their Lodge meetings

there. It was said that in a coffee house a man could "pick up more useful knowledge than by applying himself to his books for a whole month". Crucially, beer and spirits were to be had there too, to help lubricate the free exchange of news and information.

However, burgeoning coffee shops being essentially what they were, the sales of non alcoholic beverages had serious economic implications for the Exchequer and for farmers. Farmers saw tea, coffee and brandy as unwelcome competition for their wheat, barley and malt – constituents of beer - and wanted them banned. When a man was in a coffee house, he was not downing ale in an alehouse. In the 3,000 or so coffee houses operating in the land in 1675, coffee was being ordered in preference to the traditional glass of ale or gin – alcoholic beverages from which the Government received substantial tax revenues. Pascal Rosee, London coffee shop pioneer, alone sold over 600 dishes of coffee a day at the very dawn of the coffee revolution.

Women Drinking in Public

World War I also had an impact of the image of women drinking in public. In the Victorian age, female drinking in public had been taboo, a furtive activity on the margins of society which offended the rules of social decorum in the eyes of the largely male gaze which was forever controlling and judging. Traditionally places in which women drank were dank and dingy, women had lower disposable income, less time to spend that income and were often burdened by children. With all the job opportunities which the war gave hitherto restrained women a chance to prove themselves in the workplace (other than just in textiles and service) women were, for a short while, emancipated and became temporary men (See Chrystal, *Women at Work in World War II*). The word emancipated derives from "out," - man - from the Latin *manus* "hand", as in slavery, and sadly not out of the control of men (which probably amounts to much the same thing). In any event the camaraderie built up by working in factories to produce materiel and munitions for the war effort led to women drinking in groups and thus raised the profile and visibility of women drinking in public even though there was no significant increase in overall consumption or the social and medical damage it wreaked. This all coincided with attempts to improve the public house (by the 'improvers') generally, a corollary to which was making pubs 'respectable enough [for women] to enter without embarrassment' (Haydon p. 284). Once in, it was not unreasonable then to expect women to go to the bar and order a drink - something which the improvers could not really argue was unseemly.

CLOSING TIME

Now, '*Will someone take me to a pub?*'

G.K. Chesterton (1874-1936)

Image by kind permission of the artist, Yvette Earl;
for lots more of her work see www.yvette-earl.com

Appendix 1: 'Newcastle landlords'

At the end of the 19th century prolific songwriter and concert hall singer William Watson (1796–1840) composed a song celebrating the landlords and landladies of Newcastle (1834) - an achievement which presumably indicates more than a passing acquaintance with the pubs of the city. "Dance To Thy Daddy" was his most celebrated song. Most were published in *Fordyce's Newcastle Song Book,* or *Tyne-side Songster* of 1842. He was also a political activist, who, at election times, turned to writing election songs in support of the candidates he preferred. Here are some excerpts which give a flavour of the piece:

'An interesting list of names and characteristic descriptions. Kind friends and acquaintance, attention I claim. While a few jolly landlords in this town I name; In alphabet order my song it is penned, And I hope, for joke's sake, it will never offend.

Chorus

Then hey for good drinking, It keeps us from thinking. We all love a drop in our turn.

A stands for Armfield, a good hearty blade.

Tho' he's left the Nag's Head, still follows his trade;

At the foot of the Market you'll find his new shop,

Where many an old friend still calls in for a drop.

B Stands for Burns, of the Theatre square;

She's an orderly woman — good drink is sold there;

If I wanted a wife, I should readily choose

This amiable widow to govern my house.

C stands for Cant, sign of the Blue Bell,

Who keeps a good house, and good porter doth sell;

Quarrelling or fighting is there seldom seen,

She's a canty old widow, but rather too keen.

D for Dixon, who once kept the Unicorn — Ho !

And **D** stands for Dixon, White Hart, you well know;

Then there's Dixon, Quayside, just a little way down —

Were the three fattest landlords in all the whole town.

E stands for Eggleton, Fighting Cocks Inn,

Tho' old, took a young wife, and thought it no sin;

F for Finlay, his shop's corner of Pudding Chare,

And good wine and spirits you'll always get there.

H for Hall, near Nuns* Gate keeps a snug oyster shop;

H stands for Horn, and he's done very weal.

Since he bother'd the heart of sly Mrs. NeiL

I stands for Inns — we've the best in the North,

There's the King's Head, the Queen's Head, the George, and the Turf;

The old Crown and Thistle, and Miller's Half Moon,

Well known to the trav'lers who frequent the town.

K Stands for Kitchen, Hell's Kitchen 'twas nam'd,

And long for good ale and good spree has been fam'd;

In each parlour, in vestry, or kitchen you'll find

The beer drawer, Mary, obliging and kind.

M stands for Mitford — he kept the North Pole,

Just over the Leazes, a dull-looking hole;

Now our favourite poet lives at Head on the Side,

Here's success to his muse — long may she preside.

P stands for Pace, sign of the White Swan,

Who, for to oblige, will do all that he can;

A convenient house, when you marketing make.

To pop in and indulge yourself with a beef-steak.

S for Sayers, Nag's Head — he keeps good mountain dew;

Only taste it, you'll find what I tell you is true.

Sure you all know the Custom-House on the Sandhill

Robin Hood, Dog and Cannon, and Tiger for me,

The Peacock well known to the clerks on the Quay;

The Old Beggar's Opera for stowrie, my pet,

Mrs. Richardson's was — and she cannot be bet.

There's the Black Bull, and Grey Bull, well known to a few;

Black, White, and Grey Horse, and Flpng Horse too.

The Black House, the White House, The Hole in the Wall,

And the Seven Stars, Pandon, if you dare to call

There's the Turk's Head, Nag's Head, and Old Barley Mow,

The Bay Horse, the Pack Horse, and Teasdale's Dun Cow:

The Ship and the Reel, the Half-Moon and the Sun;

But I think, my good friends, it is time to be done.

Then, each landlord and landlady, wish them success.

Town and trade of the Tyne, too — we cannot do less;

And let this be the toast when we meet to regale —

"May we ne'er want a bumper of Newcastle ale."

Hell's Kitchen was a notorious establishment in the Flying Horse in the Groat Market. Here is where the 'eccentric characters of Newcastle met'. My sort of pub.

Appendix 2: The Newcastle Eccentrics of 'Hell's Kitchen'

This wonderful artwork hangs in the Laing Art Gallery, Newcastle

Eccentric Characters of Newcastle by Henry Perlee Parker (after), c) Laing Art Gallery; Supplied by The Public Catalogue Foundation.

Joanna Major gives a character by character description of the eccentrics at georgianera.wordpress.com

Many of the fourteen depicted here feature in popular local ballads and folk songs. They were well known on the Newcastle streets and on the quayside, and in the alehouses. Left to right we have:

Old (or Aud) Judy Dowlings was the keeper of the Newcastle upon Tyne 'hutch', a form of strongbox used by the City Treasurer. She was a formidable guard, wielding a hefty stick in its defence... Peering over Old Judy's shoulder is **Jenny Ballo** and beside her **Whin Bob, or Robert Cruddace.** The dog is Timour, belonging to **Doodum Daddum.**

Next is **Jacky Coxon** who is mentioned in a song written by Robert Emery... called 'The Pitman's Dream – or a description of the North Pole'. The others are **Pussy Willy, Cull (or Cully) Billy and Donald**. Cully (also known as Silly Billy) was really William Scott and lived in St John's poorhouse and was the subject of various local folk songs. He lived with his diminutive mother who was only 4ft tall and who made her living as a hawker. Both mother and son were often cruelly ridiculed but Cully was a gentle man with a good nature and a quick sense of humour. He died in the poorhouse on the 31st July 1831 at the age of 68 years. Donald, obviously a Scotsman from his tartan tam o'shanter, also reveled in the name Lousy Donald.

The next four gentleman here are **Bugle-Nosed Jack, Hangy (or Hangie), Bold Archy (or Airchy) and Blind Willie**. Bugle-Nosed Jack was also known as Cuckoo Jack and Bold Archy was really Archibald Henderson, a huge, well-built man but absolutely a gentle giant, devoted to his mother who often had to lead him away from fights as he was a magnet for trouble due to his size. He died, on the 14th May 1828, at the age of 86 years. Blind Willie, or William Purvis, was probably the best known of the Newcastle Eccentrics...his father John was a waterman and his mother Margaret lived to a grand old age, dying in All Saints poorhouse at well over 100 years of age. Blind Willie (blind from birth or from very early in his childhood) was a fiddler, song writer and performer, often to be found in ale houses where he asked for a drink and entertained the regulars. He was a great favourite on the streets of Newcastle, renowned for never wearing a hat, no matter what the weather, having got fed up of it being stolen from his head by idle boys. Like his mother, he ended up in the All Saints' poorhouse where he died on the 20th July 1832 aged 80.

Finally, we have **Shoe-tie Anty, 'Captain' Benjamin Starkey and Doodem Daddum**, owner of Timour the dog. Benjamin Starkey, extremely short in stature, had pretensions to grandeur, hence his appellation of 'Captain', and certainly had some education as he was noted as a very neat writer. In his youth he had been an usher at a school, William Bird's Academy in Fetter Lane in Holborn, London (where the essayist Charles Lamb remembered him from). He was born around 1757 and died on the 9th July 1822, and was an inmate of both Freeman's Hospital and the poorhouse. Doodum Daddem is identified as John Higgins in an eprint from Nottingham University, a jack-of-all-trades and also the Town Crier or Bellman of Newcastle Upon Tyne. However, from census records, John Higgins would appear to be too young to be the man in the painting.

Joanna Major tells us that 'Woodcuts of Blind Willie and 'Captain' Benjamin Starkey appear in *Allan's Illustrated Version of Tyneside Songs*, in which many of the Newcastle Eccentrics are named. It also provides an engraving of the Hell's Kitchen portrait with a key underneath to the identities of the people within it.

Appendix 3: A Timeline of Pub law and its Social Impact and Effect

Much of the following derives from teaching.shu.ac.uk

'alcohol-related legilsation...reads like a roll-call of crisis-points in English history'

- Nicholas Dorn, *Alcohol, Youth and the State*

What this timeline does is usefully and importantly place into context much of the book's descriptions of the pubs included in the text. Not only does it explain what happened to the 'pub', it explains why, largely through legislation. At the same time it is a social history of pubs and inns in Newcastle and in Great Britain generally; it is at the same time a social history of Britain and its leisure and hospitality through the ages from the 10th century to the 21st century.

959 '"And there shall be one system of measurement, and one standard of weights such as in use in London and Winchester." A. J. Robertson considers that the reference to measurement may in fact mean capacity. If his assumption is correct it means that from 959 onwards the whole country came under the same system of capacity measurement, which was an important milestone. The matter is referred to again some 250 years later in *Magna Carta*.' (Monckton, Ale, p.34).

'Edgar was also responsible for the introduction of pegs. The drinker was limited to drinking down to a peg inserted inside the drinking horn, but this just gave rise to drinking contests - an early example of how drink legislation can back-fire. Possibly it also is the origin of the phrase, 'to take someone down a peg'. Description of 'King Edgar's Ordinance Against Drinking' in Pierce Penniless, p.106 in *The Unfortunate Traveller...*, Penguin, 1972.

997 '...King Aethelred II issued his third code of laws which were concerned with the penalties for breaches of the peace. One of these specifically refers to trouble in ale-houses: 'In the case of breach of the peace in an ale-house six half marks shall be paid in compensation if a man is slain, and twelve ores if no one is slain." (Monckton, *Ale*, p.36).

1042-1066 'Bracton tell us of a regulation of Edward the Confessor that if any man lay a third night in an inn he was called a third-night-awn-hinde, that is to say, he was looked upon in the same light as a servant of the house would be, and the host was answerable for him if he committed any offence...' (Bickerdyke, p.185).

1102 Decree from Bishop Anselm: 'Let no priest go to drinking bouts, nor drink to pegs'. (Monckton, *Ale,* p.39).

1188 Henry II introduces first national levy on the malt liquor trade. Used to finance the Crusade against Saladin: payment of one tenth of 'moveables' [stock-in-trade]. Known as the Saladin Tithe. (Monckton, *Public*, p.19).

1189 City Council, concerned about fire hazards: '...that all alehouses be forbidden except those which shall be licensed by the Common Council of the City at Guildhall, excepting those belonging to persons who will build of stone, that the city may be secure. And that no baker bake, or ale-wife brew by night, either with reeds or straw or stubble, but with wood only.' (Monckton, *Public*, pp.18-19).

1200 Earliest statute of foreign wine trade. Anjou wines not to be sold for more than 24s a tun, Poitou wines no higher than 20s. Other French wines limited to 25s. Twelve honest men in each town to superintend the assize. (French, p.78. His source is Holinshed).

1215 *Magna Carta*, Article No. 35, 'There shall be standard measures for wine, ale and corn...'

1266 'The Assize of Ale in 1266 was the first government attempt to regulate ale prices and reflected the Crown's concern to peg them to the price of corn.' [Monckton, *Ale*, appendix]

1276 Assize. 'A gallon of ale to be sold for three farthings and another for a penny and no dearer.' First suggestion 'that two grades of ale at different prices could be sold to the public' (Monckton, *Public,* p.21).

1277 Assize. 'And that no brewster henceforth sell except by true measures viz., the gallon, the pottle [half gallon] and the quart. And that they be marked by the seal of the Alderman, and that the tun be of 150 gallons and sealed by the Alderman.' 'This appears to be the first statutory reference to the need for brewsters to have properly stamped measures for selling large or small quantities of ale.' (Monckton, *Public*, p.21).

1283 'subsequent royal ordinance set the price for better-quality ale at 1d. a gallon and weaker drink at 1d.'

1285 'By the Statuta Civitatis London., passed in 1285, taverns were forbidden to remain open after curfew in the metropolis.' (Monckton, *History*)

1309 London population stands at 30-40,000. With 354 taverns, mainly wine, over 1330 'brewshops, brewing and retailing ale' (Monckton, *History* p.21).

1315 'Edward II ordered all taverns in London not to sell wine above 3d. a gallon.'

1330 Because there are more taverners in the realm than were wont to be, selling as well corrupt wines as wholesome, and have sold the gallon at such price as they themselves would, because there was no punishment ordained for them, as hath been for them that sell bread and ale, to the great hurt of the people,' that wine must be sold at reasonable prices, and that the wines should be tested twice a year - at Easter and Michaelmas, oftener if needful - and corrupt wines poured out, and the vessels broken.' (French, pp.106-7).

1338 Wine taxed, 'on a great emergency', because Edward III 'wanted a vast sum to pay the subsidies which he had granted to his foreign allies.' (French, p.107).

1365 Act. "The King wills of his grace and sufferance that all merchant denizens that be not artificers, shall pass into Gascoign to fetch wines thence, to the end and intent that by this general licence greater liberty may come, and greater market may be of wines within the realm; and that the Gascoigns and other aliens may come into the realm with their wines, and freely sell them without any disturbance or impeachment." (French, p.107).

1369 ? 42 Edward III, c.8. 'wines forbidden to be brought into England save by Gascons and other aliens.' (French, p.107). Act renewed the following year by his son the Prince.

1375 'In London in 1375 it was ordered that no brewer should have a pole bearing his sign which projected more than seven feet over the highway.' (Monckton, *History*, p.52)

1378 'foreigners allowed to sell wine in gross but not in retail' (French, p.107).

1381 'no sweet wines or claret could be sold retail' (French, p.108).

1387 'no wine to be carried out of the realm', (French, p.108).

1393 'Richard II ordered that alehouses must exhibit a sign. This law included the following words: "Whosoever shall brew in the town with intention of selling it must hang out a sign, otherwise he shall forfeit his ale." Connected with the statutory obligation of summoning an ale-taster to which reference has already been made [1330].' (Monckton, *Public*)

From the reign of Henry VI (1422-1461) onwards, beer begins to replace ale, according to Bickerdyke, p.68 and p.143.

1450 Nottingham alehouses to close at 9.00pm

1485 Henry VII passes a law, 'that no Gascony or Guienne wines should be imported into any part of his dominions,' unless in English, Irish or Welsh ships using E, I or W sailors', (French, p.126).

1492 7 Henry VII, c.7. - '(in order to counteract the duty of four ducats a tun lately imposed by the Venetians) that 'every merchant stranger (except English born) bringing malmseys into this realm, should pay 18s. custom for each butt, over and above the custom aforetime used to be paid.' The price of the butt was fixed at 4l.'

1496 'Two justices of Peace may reject common selling of Ale, etc.' [Statutes at Large 1494. 1496?]

1531 'By an Act of 1531, every brewer was forbidden to take more than such prices and rates as should be thought sufficient, at the discretion of Justices of Peace within every shire, or by the mayor and sheriffs in a city.' (French, p.137).

'In the year 1531, brewers were forbidden to make the barrels in which their ale was sold.' (Bickerdyke).

1532 23 Henry VIII, c.7, 'the wines of Gascony and Guienne were forbidden to be sold above eightpence the gallon, and the retail price of 'Malmeseis, romenies, sakkes, and other swete wynes,' was fixed at 12d. the gallon, 6d. the pottle, 3d. the quart...' (French, p.137).

1552 5 + 6 Edward VI, c.25. 'For Keepers of Alehouses and Tiplinghouses to be bound by Recognisance'. '...Parliament requires all alehouses to have a licence from the justices of the peace' (p.41) [JPs allowed to select from time to time 'at their discretion' who could keep an alehouse', Webbs, p.7]. Act 'specifically exempted retailing at fairs from its provisions'. Execution of it inconsistent and evasion widespread (Clark, 169-170).

Now we start to see distinctions between drinking-places and places offering accommodation for travellers, when a law forbids 'innkeepers to have local people drinking in their houses, and alehouses were not licensed to have guests sleeping on the premises'. Also 'The legislation suppressing monastery activity in 1539 upset the widespread system of monks keeping "open house", often a separated "guest house". The independent inn was thus encouraged.' (*The Pub and the People*, p.81).

'In the reign of Edward VI., by the Statute 5 and 6 Ed. VI. c. 5 (repealed 5 Eliz. c. 2), it was enacted that all land formerly in tillage should again be cultivated, excepting "land set with saffron or hops."', (Bickerdyke, p.73).

1553 7 Edward 6, c.5. 'The Act to avoid the excessive Prices of Wine'. Act restricts number of taverns and who can sell wine; ale houses not allowed to sell wine.

1577 Government survey for fiscal purposes, over 30 counties. 17,595 drinking houses: 86% classed as alehouses, 12% as inns; 2% as taverns. From this we can extrapolate 24,000 alehouses for a population of 3.4 million = one alehouse per 142 inhabitants.

1580s Tobacco introduced by Raleigh.

1590 22 Elizabeth I, "that no innkeeper, common brewer, or typler shall keep in their houses any fewel, as straw or verne, which shall not be thought requisite, and being warned of the constable to rid the same within one day, subpna, xxs." The act was 'nominally against the danger of fire, but in reality it was intended to prevent tipplers from having the means of conducting furtive brewings'. (French, p.146).

1603 First legislation against drunkenness appears in James I's reign - appears to have little effect, and alehouses remained crowded, (Wrightson, p.6).

'regulations were made for the curing of hops, which process had thenceforward to be carried out under the inspection of the officers of excise.' (Bickerdyke, p.73)

1604 2(1) Jac. I, c.9., 'An Act to restrain the inordinate Haunting and Tipling of Inns, Alehouses, and other Victualling Houses'.

1606 4 Jac. I, c.5, 'An Act for repressing the odious and loathsome Sin of Drunkenness'.

1604-10 'Legislation in 1604 specifically permitted labourers and handicraftsmen to stop work for an hour at dinner time "to take their diet in an alehouse. In 1606-7 there were acts against drunkenness and against brewers selling to unlicensed tipplers, with further regulation in 1610.' Mainly tinkering with the 1552 Act. (Clark, p.172)

1618 James I. Sunday hours 1st legislated - 'closure of alehouses during the hours of divine services' (Barr, p.148).

1619 14 January, Royal Proclamation: 'alehouse keepers were to be bound in recognizances of 10 and had to find two sureties willing to be bound in 5 apiece' (Ashton, p.11), and strict guidelines on conditions of running their businesses.

1620 Feb 1620, Court of Aldermen allow chandlers to sell ale and beer (Ashton, p.12)

1623 21 Jac. I, c.7. Repression of drunkenness, and restraint of haunting.

1627 3 Charles I. '...a fine of twenty shillings, or whipping, is imposed for keeping an ale-house without a licence.' (French, p.206)

Late 1630s *the beer bottle is born.*

1638   The retailing of wine in bottles prohibited. Bottling was necessary for light wines, which will not keep in a cask, and the act thus probably led to adulteration, (French, p.206). 'A Parliamentary Ordinance issued on 16 May 1643 imposed a duty rate of 2/- a barrel on all beer, including that brewed domestically, having a value of over 6/- a barrel. In July and September of the same year other articles were added to the Excise list.' (Monckton, *History*, p.116).

1645   Charles I at Oxford issues a warrant stating that he will levy the same duty on beer as that levied by Parliament. (Monckton, p.116).

1650   Tax on a barrel of strong beer 2s 6d. (Askwith, p.12).

1652   First bag of coffee brought to England; 'it was a new drink for Pepys in 1661' However - 'In 1650 was opened at Oxford the first coffee-house by Jacobs, a Jew, at the Angel, in the parish of St. Peter in the East; and there it was, by some who delighted in novelty, drunk. Hence the antiquary Oldys is incorrect in stating that the use of coffee in England was first known in 1657.' (French, p.215). See Chrystal, *Coffee*.

   General use of coffee, according to John Evelyn (Diary) is 1667, although notes, May 1637, ''one Nathaniel Conopios, out of Greece, from Cyrill, the Patriarch of Constantinople, was the first he ever saw drink coffee'.' (French, p.231).

1657   Chocolate introduced, and tea in about 1660 (Monckton, *Public*, p.55, but see 1659). See Chrystal, *A History of Chocolate* and Chrystal, *Tea*.

   Excise officers have powers of entry, search, and seizure of goods. (Monckton, *History*, p.117).

1659   'Rugge's Diurnal mentions Coffee, Chocolate, "and a kind of drink called Tee [sic], sold in almost every street in 1659."' [*Roxburghe Ballads*, V., p.173]

1660   Pepys entry, 28 Sept. 1660, 'I did send for a cup of tea (a China drink) of which I had never drank before' - (Monckton, Public, 55). Popularised by Charles II's wife, Catharine of Braganza, (French, p.231).

1672   [Check date] 12 Car. II., c.25. Wine Act. (French, p.233). Price of wines fixed. Also gives a list of types of adulteration.

1673   Petition asking for the prohibition of 'brandy, coffee, mum, tea, and chocolate'. The petition notes that brandy has now become a very common drink. (Bickerdyke, p.118).

1689   1 W + M c.24. 'An Act for an additional Duty of Excise upon Beer, Ale, and other Liquors.' To last 3 years.

1 W+M c.34. 'An Act for prohibiting all Trade and Commerce with France.' Mainly targeted at the importation of wine and brandy.

'Partly through hostility to France, and partly to encourage the home distilleries, the Government of the Revolution, in 1689, prohibited the importation of spirits from all foreign countries, and threw open the distillery trade, on payment of certain duties to all its subjects. These measures laid the foundation of the great extention of the English manufacture of spirits. Any person was permitted to set up a distillery, on giving ten days' notice to the excise.' (French, p.245).

1690 2 William + Mary. Session 2. c.3 (13) [i.e., if numbers run on consecutively from Session 1]. 'An Act for doubling the Duty of Excise upon Beer, Ale, and other Liquors, during the Space of One Year.'

2 W + M ss2 c.9 (19). 'An Act for the encouraging the Distilling of Brandy and Spirits from Corn, and for laying several Duties on Low Wines, or Spirits of the First Extraction.'

2 William + Mary. Session 2. c.10 (20). 'An Act for granting to their Majesties several additional Duties of Excise upon Beer, Ale, and other Liquors, for Four Years...' In order to protect trade, build up the navy and maintain the war against France.

Consumption of gin, 0.5m gallons [5m gallons in 1729 - Kinross]

1694 population of England and Wales, six million

'Any Person may distil for Sale Low Wines from Drink brewed from malted Corn, & c. paying the Duties.'

First restrictions on opening times introduced in the 18th century.

London is 4th largest city in the world after Constantinople, Peking and Edo (modern Tokyo).

1702 1 Anne Stat.2 c.14. 'An Act for encouraging the Consumption of malted Corn, and for the better preventing the running of French and Foreign Brandy.' No necessity for distillers to take licenses as common Alehouse Keepers as long as they 'do not permit or suffer Tippling in his or their Houses.' Repeals clause in 12+13 W3 c.11.18.

['An Act for the incouraging the consumption of malted corn and for the better preventing the running of French and Foreign Brandy' (Simon)]

1703 (?) The Methuen Treaty - wines from Portugal admitted into England at 7 a tun, whereas French wines admitted at 55 per tun.

1720 Mutiny Act. 'all retailers who were also distillers or whose principal dealings' were more 'in other goods and merchandize than in brandy and strong waters' and who did not 'suffer tippling in their houses' were exempted from the burdensome obligation to have soldiers quartered upon them which was laid upon inn-keepers, keepers of livery stables, victuallers and retailers of strong waters within the Bills of Mortality.' (George, p.43)

1721 'the beginning of the campaign against gin-drinking'. (George, p.44)

1729 'the Grand Jury of Middlesex presented geneva-shops as a nuisance' (George, p.46).

Gin taxed and a license required by retailers (Kinross)

First attempt at legislation on spirits trade - 'Retailers were required to purchase an annual excise license costing 20...'. Fails miserably.

Duty of 2s. a gallon on compound spirits.

'any two justices had the power to grant a licence and until 1729 were free to do so at any time of the year. After this date the well-known *Brewster Sessions* were instituted when licences could only be granted at a General Sessions of the Justices of the division, one of which was to be held in September of each year.' Monckton, *Public*, p.37.

1730s *'In the 1730s the excise on the drink trade yielded a quarter of national revenue from taxation'*, Clark, p.185.

Hogarth's prints for the Stages of Cruelty appeared on 21 February 1751, a week after Beer Street and Gin Lane were issued graphically showing the social perils of alcohol. William Hogarth (1697–1764)

Gin Lane 1751 - Copper plate (etched and engraved) The Metropolitan Museum of Art, Rogers Fund, 1921, 21.55.3

1743 Quantity of spirits sold peaks at 8 million gallons. (George, p.48).

16 Geo. II c.8. 'An Act for repealing certain Duties on Spirituous Liquors, and on Licenses for retailing the same, and for laying other Duties on Spirituous Liquors, and on Licenses to retale [sic] the said Liquors.' A licence granted for 1 payable to the Excise, to be given 'to such Persons only who shall keep Taverns, Victualling-houses, Inns, Coffee-houses, or Ale-houses...'

'In 1743 Parliament abandoned its attempt to suppress the popular trade in spirits. Instead it endeavoured to annex the retailing of gin and brandy to the respectable world of the victualling house.' (p.242)

17 Geo. II c.17 and 19. 'Licences only to be granted to keepers of public houses for that one house only'. (Monckton, *Public,* 65). 17 Geo. II c. 17 and 19. 'Licence holders not to be grocers, chandlers or distillers'.

24 Geo. II and 26 Geo. II c.31 s.9. 'Justices protected against writs and also given summary powers of search'. (Monckton, *Public,* p.65). [Possibly in this Act] a clause 'forbidding spirits to be sold in prisons' - although ignored (George, p.291; and Ch.1 n.41).

'The Act of 1751 really did reduce the excesses of spirit-drinking. It was a turning-point in the social history of London and was so considered when this time was still within living memory.' (George, p.49).

1753 'In 1753 Parliament passed a law requiring all clerks of the peace to keep registers of victuallers licensed in their jurisdictions.'

26 Geo. II c.31. 'Licences only to be granted at Brewster Sessions and at no other time of the year. Brewers or distillers not to be Justices'. (Monckton, Public, p.65).

26 Geo. II c.31 s.1. 'Licensee to produce sureties in his good behaving'. (Monckton, *Public,* p.65).

26 Geo. II c.31 s.16. 'Licensee to be of a much higher personal standing'. (Monckton, PH, 65.)

26 Geo. II c.31 and 29 Geo. II c.12. 'Transfer of licences tightened up'. (Monckton, PH, 65).

1754 Hardwicke's Marriage Act ends 'clandestine marriages', which often took place in taverns, eg Fleet marriages. (Earle, p.178).

The Cider Bill debated, March. Riots in 'the cider counties'.

1768 First modern hotel built in Exeter, imaginatively called the Hotel (Everitt, p.92. Alteration made and name changed to Royal Clarence Hotel, 1827).

1784 Pitt adds another 10s to the publican's licence, (Monckton, *Public*, p.67).

1801 Population of. England + Wales 8,893, 000. (first census). Number of fully licensed premises: 49,000. (Monckton, Public).

Home brewing accounts for half of total consumption. By end of century virtually nil.

1807 47 Geo. III. c. 68, an Act to prevent the abuses associated with pubs acting as houses of call and the publicans as middle-men in coal-heaving.

'This Act, ineffectual as it proved, is interesting as a piece of social legislation quite counter to laissez-faire principles, and also as an early attempt to prevent by Statute the payment of wages in public-houses.' (George, p.287)

1816 48,000 licensed alehouses in England and Wales, of which 14,200 (30%) belong to breweries, 10,800 to occupiers, 22,700 to disinterested persons. (Monckton, *Public*, p.88).

The Alehouse Act 1828. Established a general annual licensing meeting to be held in every city, town, division, county and riding, for the purposes of granting licences to inns, alehouses and victualling (the provision of food) houses to sell excisable liquors to be drunk on the premises.

The Beer House Act 1830. A failed attempt to wean drinkers of the evil gin onto beer – considered to be much healthier. A beerhouse was a type of public house created by the 1830 Beerhouse Act, legally defined as a place "where beer is sold to be consumed on the premises". They were also known as 'small' or 'Tom and Jerry' shops. Existing public houses were issued with licences by local magistrates under the terms of the Retail Brewers Act 1828, and were subject to police inspections at any time of the day or night. Proprietors of the new beerhouses, on the other hand, simply had to buy a licence from the government costing two guineas per annum, equivalent to about £150 in 2010. On payment of the two guineas the Beerhouse Act enabled any rate-payer to brew and sell beer thus increasing competition between brewers; lowering prices and encouraging people to drink beer instead of strong spirits, notably gin. It resulted in the flood gates opening as thousands of new public houses and breweries throughout the country threw open their doors, particularly in the industrial north of England. In Manchester and Salford alone there were 27 breweries in 1827, which had increased to 75 by 1873. The law permitted beer houses to sell beer although a full license was still required for the sale of wine, spirits and beers in the public ale house (pub). Beer houses were often just a room in a house where beer was sold to the bloke next door or down the street, and his wife.

A letter from the time notes: 'The new Beer Act has begun its operations. Everyone is drunk. Those who are not singing are sprawling. The sovereign people is in a beastly state.' (Sidney Smith, quoted in *The Pub and the People*, p.84).

Inevitably, it proved to be controversial, removing as it did the monopoly of local magistrates to lucratively regulate local trade in alcohol, and it did not apply retrospectively to those who already ran public houses. It was also denounced as promoting inebriation.

By 1841 licences under the new law had been issued to 45,500 commercial brewers. One detrimental effect of the Act was the dismantling of provisions for detailed recording of licences, which were only restored by subsequent regulatory legislation: the Wine and Beerhouse Act 1869 and the Wine and Beerhouse Act Amendment Act 1870. The Act was frequently amended, notably in 1834 and 1840.

'First **Temperance Societies** set up in England, with a Pledge of abstinence in the use of malted liquors.' (Carter, 249) Free-licensers set up beer halls.

1831-1881 Number of public houses rose by nearly 50% in England and Wales (Clark).

1832 Reform Bill (Sep 1).

1832 September 1. 'Entire Abstinence' Pledge, 'the seven men of Preston'. English Total Abstinence Movement (Livesey).

1834 **Second Beerhouse Act.** [Knatchbull's bill passed]. Tightens up the qualifications required of beersellers and creates a distinction between beerhouses with off- and on-licences for the first time.

1st Parliamentary inquiry into drunkenness. Parliamentary Select Committee on Intemperance reports. Chairman, James Silk Buckingham, M.P. (See French, pp.353ff, for details of recommendations).

1839 **Metropolitan Police Act**: a clause which allows for the prohibition of Sunday morning opening (first statutory regulation of public house hours). Effective and incorporated into local Improvement Acts elsewhere. (Carter) Metropolitan Police Act: forbids London drink sellers from allowing children under 16 to drink on the premises, (whole country extension, 1874)

1840 **Beer House Act**. Beerhouse rating qualifications raised. Introduces principle of varying statutory closing hours with population density. Proof required that the applicant was the 'real resident-holder or occupier of the dwelling house for which the application was being sought', Monckton, Public, p.81.

1842-8 Sunday morning closing extended throughout England.

1842 **Licensing Act** makes 'the complicated matter of the transfer of licenses from one holder to another much easier'. Monckton, Public, p.81.

1843 'In 1843 an Act was passed which at last rescued the poor coal-whippers from their 'thralldom to the publican'.' (George, p.287. Not clear if this is specific to the coal-whippers or a general act against payment of wages in alehouses).

1845 Gaming Act, 'disqualified on-licensees from allowing billiards to be played in their houses during permitted hours on Sundays, Christmas Day or Good Friday.' Monckton, Public, p.82.

1847 10 Vict., c5. The use of sugar in brewing is sanctioned. [Only previous times were 1800, 1812 and 1813 to cover agriculturally disastrous years.]

Band of Hope formed (Carter). [? See 1855]

1848 '...Lord's Day Sale of Liquors Act applied Sunday morning closing to the whole of England and Wales' (Carter).

1849-50 House of Lords Committee on Intemperance reports.

1851 Maine Law on prohibition passes.

1853 Forbes Mackenzie [Sunday closing] Act, applies to the whole of Scotland. 1st Sunday Closing legislation.

United Kingdom Alliance founded.

1854 House of Commons Select Committee on Public-Houses reports. (See French, pp.361ff for details; Askwith, Ch.4).

Act. Sunday closing: sale forbidden except between 1 and 2.30, and after 6.00, closing at 10.00, not to be re-opened until 4 am next day. 'Refreshment for bona fide travellers was permitted, and for the first time that phrase, later so great a bone of contention, found its way into the statute book.' (Askwith, p.53).

1855 Act. 1854 Act 'lightened'. On Sunday to be closed between 3 and 5; closing time to be 11. (Askwith, p.53).

UK Band of Hope formed'

1860 **Refreshment Houses Act**. Gladstone wine-licensing legislation ('grocer's licence'). Attempt to 'popularize the drinking of light foreign wines and to bring together the functions of eating and drinking.' (Monckton, *Public*, p.82).

1862 Church of England Total Abstinence Society founded, 'which rested on a broader basis than the Alliance, and more truly represented the British flair for compromise' (Askwith, pp.68-9).

1863 Sunday Closing Bill. Proposal for prohibition of 'all sale of intoxicating liquors between 11 p.m. on Saturday and 6 a.m. on Monday. Rejected. (Askwith, p.68).

Church of England Total Abstinence Society drops the 'Total' from its title. 'A few years later it dropped the "Reformation" from its title, and ever since has been content with the word "Temperance" to denote the special ground on which it takes its stand' (Askwith, p.69).

1868 **Sunday Closing Bill**. Proposal to prohibit 'all Sunday sales for drinking on the premises, but to allow "dinner and supper beer" for home consumption to be purchased during certain hours'. Rejected. (Askwith, p.68).

'A short Bill was submitted in 1868 to the Home Secretary by an influential deputation, on which the Roman Catholics were represented by Archbishop, afterwards Cardinal, Manning, supported by other religious and moderate reforming bodies, which provided that after a certain date no fresh licenses should be granted under the 1830 Act. As these licenses had hitherto been purely personal, they would practically have been extinguished in ten or fifteen years.' (Askwith, p.72).

1869 **The Wine and Beer House Act.** An attempt to get the genie back in the bottle, allowing magistrates to refuse the renewal of licences or granting new licences. *If you want to know when the decline in British pubs started, then this is it.*

'The main provision [of the Act] ... was to transfer the issue of beer-house licenses from the Excise, by whom they had been issued since 1830, to the magistracy, who were thenceforward enabled to exercise the same discretionary power in the case of applications for new beer and wine licenses as they already exercised in the case of spirit licenses...' / Effect is to reduce the number of licences, but, by increasing the value of licences, encourage the 'tied-house' system because more investment by brewers in the retail trade (Askwith, pp.72-3).

1874 Licensing Act. Forbidden for drink sellers to allow children under 16 to drink on the premises.

British Women's Temperance Association founded.

1878 Act. Sunday closing in Ireland.

1879 [Dr. Cameron's] [First] Habitual Drunkards Act 'required that a number of retreats be set up for the admission of voluntary patients who were addicted to alcoholic drinks.' Patients had to pay for their own treatment. After agreeing to treatment, patient 'statutorily obliged to remain for the full period of the cure.' (Monckton).

1881 Sunday Closing (Wales) Act. [Note - England now the odd one out, although a Bill gained a second Commons reading, but rejected].

1896 First Royal Commission on Licensing Laws appointed.

The Crown Temperance Hotel, 15-17 Grey Street

19th Century Engraving Robinson Library Special Collections, Accession number: ILL/11/188

Robinson Library Newcastle University

© Copyright 2013 Newcastle University

Barfight in 'The Spoilers'. John Wayne winning.

1898 Second Habitual Drunkards Act. Magistrates given 'power to commit criminal inebriates to special reformatories'. (Monckton, *Public*, p.85.)

   End of century, convictions for drunkenness running at 65 for each 10,000 of population, of which one fifth were females. (Monckton, *Public*, p.86.)

1901 Intoxicating Liquor (Sale to Children) Act. Also known as the Child Messenger Act. Sale of beer to children under 14 is prohibited.

Population of England and Wales: 32,528,000. Number of fully licensed premises: 102,000 (Monckton, *Public*).

Licensing Act. 'An Act to amend the law relating to the sale of Intoxicating Liquors and to Drunkenness, and to provide for the Registration of Clubs'.

'The police were given power to arrest anyone found drunk in the streets or any public place, including licensed premises, whilst in charge of a child under seven years of age. The husband or wife of a habitual drunkard was enabled to obtain a maintenance or separation order, and under certain circumstances a drunken wife could be committed to a retreat for inebriates. The sale of intoxicants to habitual drunkards was prohibited.' (Monckton, *Public*, p.101).

1908 **Asquith Licensing Bill**, 'which he described as having two main purposes, namely, "an immediate and progressive reduction in the excessive facilities which are now allowed for the sale of intoxicating drinks," and "the gradual, but complete, recover, with due regards for existing interests, by the State of its dominion over, and its property in, a monopoly which has been improvidently allowed to slide out of its control". (Askwith, p.185). Passes the Commons by majority, rejected by the Lords.

Children's Act. '...an offence to give intoxicants to children under the age of five except in an emergency or upon the orders of the doctor.' Children under 14 not allowed in licensed bars during opening hours.

1914 Initially the naval and military authorities are given powers to restrict hours of sale in or near harbours and in other areas.

August 31. Intoxicating Liquor (Temporary Restriction) Act (similar powers to those granted to the naval and military authorities). To last for the duration of the war and for one month afterwards.

'The war affected the production and consumption of alcoholic liquors in every country by the withdrawal of materials for manufacture in order to make good the deficiency of food, by interference with transport, and by increase of prices. These changes caused a general, though unequal, diminution of production and consumption.' / '... in Great Britain a system of control was instituted which placed the trade in all its branches on a wholly different legal footing, changed its practice in many important respects, and introduced far-reaching experiments. In this procedure Great Britain stood quite alone. Prohibition, adopted in Norway in 1916, was rather the culmination of a long-standing campaign than a war measure; and the same may be said of its adoption during the war in the Canadian provinces and Newfoundland. The war no doubt stimulated a movement already in progress, as it did in the United States, where national prohibition came into force in 1911; but the action in Great Britain was quite new and totally different.' (Shadwell, *Drink*, p.ix)

Restrictions promptly enforced. 'The hours of sale were shortened at both ends;

in the morning by fixing the time for opening at 8 A.M. or 9 A.M. instead of 6 A.M., and in the evening by closing an hour or two hours earlier. In London the closing time was shortened on September 4 from 12.30 A.M. to 11 P.M., and on October 19 to 10 P.M.' (Shadwell, *Drink,* p.4).

War tax on beer imposed November 18 1914, to raise revenue rather than curtail drinking.

[Writing in 1943] 'The last war transformed pub-life. There were drastic restrictions upon the hours during which could be open, drastic increases in the price of drink (between 1914 and 1921 duty on each barrel of beer rose from 7s. 9d. to 100s, a considerable decrease in the amount of beer drunk, and a 600 per cent fall in the number of convictions for drunkenness. They became accepted as pub normality. Numerous local and other restrictions (such as the "no treating" rule which was an attempt to alter the basic pattern of pub life) were temporary, and produced no post-war effects.' (*The Pub and the People*, p.12).

[Duty on beer increased as follows: 1914, 7s 9d; 1915, 23s; 1916, 23s; 1917, 24s; 1918, 25s; 1919, 50s; 1920, 70s; 1921, 100s; 1922, 100s. Duty on spirits (proof per gallon) increased from 14s 9d in 1914 to 72s 6d in 1921. Source - Shadwell, *Drink*, pp.86-7].

Convictions for drunkenness in 1914 - 183, 828; in 1918 - 29,075 (Shadwell, *Drink*, p.89).

[Note - war-time Acts are not actual licensing Acts] Defence of the Realm Act, commonly known as D.O.R.A. / 'Before the end of 1914 some 623 orders had been made under the Act.' (Monckton, PH, p.103).

1915   May 19. Defence of the Realm (Amendment) No. 3. Act creates the Central Control Board (Liquor Traffic) under the Chairmanship of Lord D'Abernon.

'This statute completely superseded the ordinary law within the defined limits and transferred the control of the trade from the local authorities to the Government, to be administered through a special organ called 'the prescribed authority.' At the same time, it conferred on this authority far wider powers of action than those previously possessed by the local magistrates.' (Shadwell, *Drink*, p.26).

'The greatest change introduced was a drastic reduction in the hours of sale. Previously these had been on week-days - in London 19½ hours, namely from 5 A. M. to 12.30 midnight (Saturdays 12 midnight); in other English towns 17 hours, namely from 6 A. M. to 11 P. M.; in country districts 16 hours, namely from 6 A.M. to 10 P.M.' - 'The Board reduced these hours at one stroke to 5½ in all districts, namely 2½ hours at midday (12 to 2.30 P. M.) And 3 in the evening (6 P.M. to 9 P.M., or 6.30 P.M. to 9.30 P.M.). Except during these hours the sale of alcoholic liquor for consumption on the premises was prohibited, and this applied to clubs as well as to licensed houses of all kinds.'

Three main changes effected by this. 1 - 'Public-house drinking in the forenoon was completely stopped', 2 - 'drinking in the evening ceased much earlier'; 3 - 'an interval of several hours was interposed in the afternoon between the morning and the evening periods of sale, so that the consumption of liquor coincided broadly with meal-times, and ceased in the intervening period.' (Shadwell, *Drink*, pp.37-8)

Lloyd George (as Chancellor of the Exchequer) had given a speech at Bangor, February 28, outlining how a minority were refusing to work a full week, because, 'let us be perfectly candid. It is mostly the lure of drink. ... Drink is doing us more damage in the war than all the German submarines put together.' (Quoted in Shadwell, *Drink*, p.12; but Shadwell also notes Lloyd George's tendency to overstate the case, as described in the *Times* leader, April 3, 1915, after George had argued that of the three enemies Germany, Austria and Drink, Drink was the most formidable).

1916 April, Beer Restriction Act, 'limiting output to 26 million barrels for the ensuing twelve months' (Shadwell, *Drink*, p.95)

1917 March - 'Beer output limited to 10 million barrels by Food Controller. Clearances of spirits from bond limited to one-half of previous year's.' (Shadwell, Drink, p.95)

1919 March - 'Weekday evening hours of sale extended half an hour by Cotnrol Board - generally to 9.30. P. M.' - further extended to 10 in May. Sunday evening hours extended in July from 9 to 10. (Shadwell, *Drink*, p.96)

1921 August 17. Licensing Act. 'Under this Act the hours during which intoxicating liquor might be sold or supplied for consumption either "on" or "off" whether in licensed premises or clubs, were limited to nine in the metropolis and eight (or eight and a half) elsewhere on weekdays, and five on Sundays, Christmas Day and Good Friday, except in Wales and Monmouthshire, where there was no Sunday opening.' Between 9 a.m. and 10 p.m. (or 10.30 p.m.; between 11 a.m. and 11 p.m. in London) 2 hours interval required. Note: there were 'no longer any statutory "closing hours" for licensed premises'. (Askwith, p.199).

1923 **Intoxicating Liquor (Sale to Persons under Eighteen) Act**. Illegal for persons under 18 yrs old to buy or serve alcoholic drinks on licensed premises, 'but allowed the sale of beer and cider with a meal to a person over sixteen years.' (Monckton, Ale, p.184).

1934 **Licensing (Permitted Hours) Act**, 'gave authority to licensing justices to extend the closing hour from 10 p.m. until 10.30. p.m. for part of a year should special circumstances or requirements dictate that it was in the public interest so to do.' (Monckton, Ale, p.184)

1950 Figures for drunkenness in England and Wales: 11 per 10,000 people each year.

Number of on-licenses in England and Wales: 73,000. Registered clubs 24,000 (from virtually 0 in 1900).

1960s Convictions for drunkenness about 15 persons per 10,000, of which a twentieth are women. Monckton, *Public Houses*, p.85.

1961 Licensing Act. Sunday opening. Ten-minute drinking up period introduced. Extension of London conditions applied in 1949 to rest of country.

The Betting, Gaming, and Lotteries Act covers the use of 'one-armed bandits' and amusement machines on licensed premises.

1967 Road Traffic Act. Introduction of the breathalyzer.

1972 Erroll Committee - recommendation to extend closing time beyond 11pm (originally introduced at the start of WW1).

1976 (Scotland) Pubs allowed to open weekday afternoons and Sunday opening.

1982 Illegal now for women to be refused service in pubs and bars

1987 Sunday opening.

1988 (England and Wales) Pubs allowed to open weekday afternoons.

1995 (England) Sunday afternoon drinking.

2023 Tax on most alcoholic drinks increased, and this in a time of increasing poverty and high inflation and interests rates and soaring fuel and energy bills. Everyone needs a break.

For much of the 19th and 20th century in the United Kingdom, the local pub was often no place for women. But that all finally ended in 1982.

FURTHER READING

Ashton, Robert, 'Popular Entertainment and Social Control in Later Elizabethan and Early Stuart London', *London Journal* 9 (1983) 3-19.

Askwith, Lord, 1928, *British Taverns. Their History and Laws*, London

Barr, Andrew, 1995. *Drink. An Informal Social History*, London

Bennison, Brian, 1991, *The Centenary History of the Newcastle Breweries Ltd., 1890-1990*, Newcastle

Bennison, Brian, *The Brewing trade in North East England 1869-1939*. Thesis submitted by Brian Robert Bennison for the degree of Doctor of Philosophy, University of Newcastle upon Tyne, July 1992

Bennison, Brian, 1995, *Brewers and Bottlers of Newcastle-upon-Tyne* from 1850 to the present day, Newcastle

Bennison, Brian, 1996, *Heady Days - A History of Newcastle's Public Houses, Vol 1, The Central Area*

Bennison, Brian, 1997, *Heavy Nights - A History of Newcastle's Public Houses, Volume Two, The North and East*

Bennison, Brian, 1998, *Lost Weekends Heavy Nights - A History of Newcastle's Public Houses, Volume Three, The West*

Bennison, Brian, 2001, Drinking in Newcastle, in Colls, Robert, *Newcastle upon Tyne: A modern history*, Chichester

Bickerdyke, John, 1889, *The Curiosities of Ale and Beer: An Entertaining History*, London, Swan Sonnenschein

Boothroyd, John, 2014, *The Old Pubs of Gateshead*, Newcastle

Bonney, Stewart, 2010, *50 Favourite Northumbrian Pubs*, Newcastle-upon-Tyne

Brandon, D. 2010, *Discovering Pub Names and Signs*, Oxford, 2010

Brandwood, G. 2011, *Licensed to Sell – The History and Heritage of the Public House* 2nd edition, English Heritage

Brandwood, G., 2016, Britain's Real Heritage Pubs: Pub I, nteriors of Outstanding Historic Interest, CAMRA

Bretherton, R. F., 1931, 'Country Inns and Alehouses', in Lennard, Reginald (ed) *Englishmen at Rest and Play: Some Phases of English Leisure 1558-1714*, Oxford

Brett, Alan, 2003, *Sunderland Public Houses*, Sunderland

Bruning, T. 2000, *Historic Pubs of England*, London

Camerons Brewery History. Camerons Brewery Archived 1 August 2012 at the Wayback Machine

CAMRA *Regional Inventory of the North East: Pub interiors of special historic interest*, St Albans

Carter, Henry, 1933, *The English Temperance Movement: A Study in Objectives*, London

Chatterton, Paul et al, 2001, *Changing our Toon: Youth, nightlife and urban change in Newcastle*, University of Newcastle-upon-Tyne

Chrystal, Paul, 2014, *Tea: A Very British Beverage*, Stroud

Chrystal, Paul, 2016, *Coffee: A Drink for the Devil*, Stroud

Chrystal, Paul, 2016, *Harrogate Pubs including Knaresborough*, Stroud

Chrystal, Paul 2017, *The Place Names of Yorkshire, including Pub Names*, Catrine

Chrystal, Paul, 2017, *Hull Pubs*, Stroud

Chrystal, Paul, 2018, *Pubs in and around the Yorkshire Dales*, Darlington

Chrystal, Paul, 2018, *Yorkshire Murders, Manslaughter and Madness*, Catrine

Chrystal, Paul, 2019, *Pubs in and around York*, Darlington

Chrystal, Paul, 2020, *The Place names of County Durham*, Catrine

Chrystal, Paul, 2020, *Leeds Pubs*, Stroud

Chrystal, Paul, 2022, *Factory Girls: The working lives of Women and Children*, Barnsley

Chrystal, Paul, 2023, *Women at Work in World War I and II*, Barnsley

Clark, Peter, 1983, *The English Alehouse: A Social History 1200-1830*, Harlow

Cooper, T.P., 1897, *The Old Inns and Inn Signs of York*, York 1897

Davis, B., 1981, *The Traditional English Pub: A Way of Drinking*, London

Dorn, Nicholas, 1983, *Alcohol, Youth and the State*, London

Earle, Peter, 1989, *The Making of the English Middle Class. Business, Society and Family Life in London, 1660-1730*, London

Eby, Margaret, 2019, "The rise of the sober bar". BBC.

Edman, Johan, 2015, "Temperance and Modernity: Alcohol Consumption as a Collective Problem, 1885–1913". *Journal of Social History*. 49 (1): 20–52.

Everitt, Alan, ed., 1973, *Perspectives in English Urban History*, London

French, R. V., *Nineteen Centuries of Drink in England: A History, Second Edition - Enlarged and Revised*, London, National Temperance Publication Depot. No date. [1st edition is 1884].

George, M. Dorothy, 1966, *London Life in the Eighteenth Century*, Harmondsworth

Gillett, A., 2016, *Beer and the Boro—A Perfect Match!*. In *Brewing, Beer and Pubs*, London

Girouard, 1984, M. *Victorian Pubs*, Yale

Gorham, M. 2007, *Back to the Local*, London

Gorham, M. 1950, *Inside the Pub*, London

Harrison, Brian, 1971 *Drink and the Victorians, The Temperance Question in England 1815–1872*, London

Harrison, Brian, 1973 "Teetotal Chartism". *History*. 58 (193): 193–217

Haydon, P. 1994, *The English Pub: A History*, London

Jack, Albert, 2009, *The Old Dog and Duck: The Secret Meaning of Pub Names*, London

Jennings, Paul, 2007, *The Local: a history of the English Pub*, London

Keating, Joseph,1913, "Temperance Movements". In Herbermann, Charles (ed.). *Catholic Encyclopedia*. New York

Kinross, Lord, 1959, *The Kindred Spirit: A History of Gin and of the House of Booth*, London

Lackey, Clifford, 1985, *Quality Pays: The Story of Joshua Tetley & Son*, Springwood Books

Lovibond, T.W., 1889, 'The Brewing Trade of the Tyne' in *British Association, Handbook to the Industries of Newcastle and District*, Newcastle

Major, Joanna, https://georgianera.wordpress.com/

Manders, Frank, 1973, *History of Gateshead*, Gateshead

Mcallister, Annemarie, 2016), "Temperance Periodicals". In: *The Routledge Handbook to Nineteenth-Century British Periodicals and Newspapers*, London

McKay, Marie-Louise, *The History of the Lion Brewery (Hartlepool)*

McKay, Marie-Louise, 2008, *The Lion Roars and the Monkey Bites*

Monckton, H.A., 1966, *A History of English Ale and Beer*, London

Monckton, H.A. 1969, *A History of the English Public House*, London

Monson-Fitzjohn, 1926, G.J. Quaint Signs of Olde Inns, London

Oliver, B. 1947, *The Renaissance of the English Public House*, London

Osborne, Lori, 2015, *Frances Willard and the Historic Link Between the 19th Century Women's Temperance and Suffrage Movements*, Washington

Pearson, Lynn, F. 1989, *The Northumbrian Pub - an architectural history,* Morpeth

Pearson, Lynn F., 1999, *British breweries: an architectural history*

Pepper, B. 1990, *A Haunt of Rare Souls*, Otley

Pickwell, W., 1886, *The Temperance Movement in the City of York, Its Origins, Basis and Progress*, York

Putnam, Roger, 2004, *The Beer and Breweries of Britain*, Shire Books

Race, M. *Public Houses, Private Lives: An Oral History of Life in York Pubs on the Mid-20th Century*

Redman, Nick, 1993, *The History of the Castle Eden Brewery, County* Durham (Whitbread plc, London)

Richmond, Lesley, 1990, *The Brewing Industry: A Guide to Historical Records.* Manchester

Ritchie, Berry, 1999, *Good Company, The Story of Scottish & Newcastle*, London

Rowntree, B.S., 1901, *Poverty: A Study of Town Life*, London 1901

Rowntree, Joseph, 1899, *The Temperance Problem and Social Reform;* facs. 2010

Rowntree, Joseph, 1903, *Public Control of the Liquor Trade*

Rowntree, Joseph, 1906, *The Taxation of the Liquor Trade*

Shadwell, Arthur, 1923, *Drink in 1914-1922 A Lesson in Control*, London

Shiman, Lilian L. "The Church of England Temperance Society In the Nineteenth Century." *Historical Magazine of the Protestant Episcopal Church 41*, no. 2 (1972): 179–95

Simon, Andre L., 1926, *Bottlescrew Days. Wine Drinking in England During the Eighteenth Century*, London

Steel, Charlie, *North Shields Public Houses, Inns & Taverns Part One and Part Two*, Summerhill Books

Webb, J.M. 'Vaux Breweries 100 Years at Castle Street', Issue No. 90 (June 1975)

Webb, Sidney, 1903, *The History of Liquor Licensing in England. Principally from 1700 to 1830, London* 1963 (repr) [1903].

Winskill, Peter Turner, 1881, *The Comprehensive History of the Rise and Progress of the Temperance Reformation from the Earliest Period to September 1881*, Mackie, Brewtnall

Wordsworth Reference Series: *The Dictionary of Pub Names*, London, 2006

Wood, R., 1963, *The Lion Brewery: A Short History*

Yeomans, Henry, 2014. *Alcohol and Moral Regulation: Public Attitudes, Spirited Measures and Victorian Hangovers*, London

http://mytynesidepubs.blogspot.com/

A HISTORY OF

YORK

In 101 People, Objects
And Places

Paul Chrystal

DestinWorld

also available